Vorwort

Mit dem neuen, spannenden Compact Lernkrimi können Sie Ihre Englischkenntnisse auf schnelle und einfache Weise vertiefen, auffrischen und überprüfen.
Inspector Hudson erleichtert das Sprachtraining mit Action und Humor. Er und seine mysteriösen Kriminalfälle stehen im Mittelpunkt einer zusammenhängenden Story.
Der Krimi wird auf jeder Seite durch abwechslungsreiche und kurzweilige Übungen ergänzt, die das Lernen unterhaltsam und spannend machen.
Prüfen Sie Ihr Business English in Lückentexten, Zuordnungs- und Übersetzungsaufgaben, in Buchstabenspielen und Kreuzworträtseln!
Ob im Bus oder in der Bahn, im Wartezimmer, zu Hause oder in der Mittagspause - das Sprachtraining im handlichen Format bietet die ideale Trainingsmöglichkeit für zwischendurch.
Schreiben Sie die Lösungen einfach ins Buch!
Die richtigen Antworten sind in einem eigenen Lösungsteil zusammengefasst.

Und nun kann die Spannung beginnen ...

Viel Spaß und Erfolg!

Die Ereignisse und die handelnden Personen in diesem Buch sind frei erfunden. Etwaige Ähnlichkeiten mit tatsächlichen Ereignissen oder lebenden Personen wären rein zufällig und unbeabsichtigt.

Inhalt

Story

James Hudson arbeitet als Inspector bei der legendären Polizeibehörde Scotland Yard. Er ist einer der fähigsten Männer und wird immer dann zu Rate gezogen, wenn seine Kollegen mal wieder vor einem Rätsel stehen. Seine resolute und krimibegeisterte Haushälterin Miss Paddington unterstützt ihn stets mit liebevoller Fürsorge.

Dieses Mal ermittelt Inspector Hudson in einem besonders kniffligen Fall. Beim Sportwagenhersteller A&L verschwindet ein Entwicklungsingenieur. Und zwar nicht irgendeiner, sondern der Beste. Gerade sind alle Tests für seine neue Entwicklung abgeschlossen, eine Entwicklung, die A&L an die Spitze der britischen Sportwagenhersteller bringen könnte. Ganz offensichtlich wurde der Ingenieur entführt. Aber wer steckt hinter der Entführung? Ist es ein Konkurrent von A&L oder sogar eine Person aus dem direkten Umfeld des Opfers? Inspector Hudson muss viel Fingerspitzengefühl aufbringen, um mit den Entführern zu verhandeln und stößt bei seinen Ermittlungen auf ein Netz von Intrigen ...
Wird es ihm gelingen, den Ingenieur zu befreien und die Drahtzieher zu entlarven?

Devilish Intrigues

"If that works the way it's designed to, you're going to be rich, Donny." A young engineer working for A&L, one of the leading producers of sports cars in the UK, looked at his colleague and friend. "This idea is going to revolutionize the industry. The Italians won't have a chance anymore."

"I know, Mal."

"Every sports car manufacturer will be trying to catch up with A&L."

"You're right. A&L will make a fortune, and what'll I get? Nothing. Or worse, I'll get a handshake and a 'Thanks mate, keep up the good work.'"

"No doubt they'll give you a pay rise or a promotion. Maybe they'll give you both."

"Not here," Donny says, "they're too cheap, always looking at the bottom line. Most companies today are only looking for short-term profit, not long-term success. If you can keep them out of the red, they keep you. If not, they sack you; send you on your way."

"It's a hard life –"

"– and then you die. Hopefully before they have to pay your pension."

He shook his head, his curly blond hair moving as if with a life of its own.

Malcolm Evans, a dark young man, whose Indian mother had inspired a strong work ethic, didn't quite agree with Donny. Donald Award, however, was a genius, with all the impatience and egotism that goes with it. Still, he and Mal often enjoyed a few rounds at the pub together or watched a football match when they could get tickets.

Übung 1: Ergänzen Sie die Sätze!

1. A person qualified to design, build or construct machines is called an engineer.
2. An employee who is paid a higher wage received a ~~promotion~~ pay-rise
3. A person in an office who is raised to a higher rank received a promotion.
4. A company trying to make a profit has to ________________.
5. A person dismissed from employment is Sacked.
6. The payment made by the government to people above a certain age is called a pension.
7. Somebody earning a lot of money with his business is ~~succes~~ successful.

Several months later.

"What do you think, Jack? It's the most important development in car engines since fuel injection," said Award. "Every test has been a complete success, ever since we solved the problems we had at the beginning. It's ready for some real road tests."

"Not so fast, Donny," said his boss, Jack Donleavy. "There have been a few successful tests, but there's more to do before this goes into production."

Award and Donleavy were standing in front of a new kind of engine, one that made sports cars capable of reaching 200 mph. It was a relatively small engine but very powerful.

Übung 2: Unterstreichen Sie im Text die englische Übersetzung der Wörter in Klammern!

(1. wirtschaftlich, 2. Motor, 3. Ruf, 4. funktionieren, 5. aufrechterhalten, 6. Zeitraum, 7. ununterbrochen, 8. Durchbruch)

"We've got to test it to see how it performs when it runs for hours at a time and to see how the engines function over a longer period," Donleavy explained. "We can't just start producing it and shipping cars with this engine all over the world."

"Why not? It's not complicated. Soon A&L could be the leading sports car producer, not just in England but throughout the world."

"What if the life of this engine is only two or three years? What if it can't maintain high speeds for hours at a time?"

"But it can. That's what we've been doing," Award almost yelled, his frustration visible on his red face. "We've tested it for months now. We haven't had to change anything major. And as for this engine having a short life span, there's absolutely no reason why it should. The materials are the same, simply used more economically."

"I believe in this, Donny. Don't get me wrong. We have to be a bit more conservative than you want. We just can't rush it onto the market, as much as you or I might like that. If something goes wrong, A&L's reputation will suffer. There's nothing harder to do than to get back a good reputation."

"We know it works. These will be high quality engines."

"It always looks so certain and then something goes wrong," said Donleavy, putting his arm on the young man's shoulders. "Come on, let's get a cup of tea," he said, directing Award towards the office.

"This is a breakthrough, Jack. Do you see that?"

"Naturally, Donny. You've done wonderful work, but I also see that there's more work to do."

The entire week, Donald Award argued with his boss and his colleagues about his innovation. It had been tested. A&L should be producing cars with the new engine, if only a few prototypes, so these cars could be driven around London – that sort of testing he could agree with. It seemed silly to keep repeating the same tests month after month. The new engine had been refined, and it was ready, he argued, for real tests – on the real streets of London, on the motorways of England, on the *Autobahn* in Germany, where drivers could really see what this new engine was capable of.

Inspector James Hudson was off-duty, leaning over his Bentley's idling engine. Though it was a Saturday afternoon, it was a rare afternoon free.

"I'm rather amazed that your Bentley's still running, James."

"Miss Paddington, this car wouldn't dare stop running. It's a question of honour. A Bentley doesn't just break down. It says, "I say, old chap, do you mind if I just have a quick lie-down right here on the M1?"

"Such nonsense. Come in and drink your tea."

"I'm just about done here," he said, looking over the engine.

"You don't know anything about motors, James."

"True, Miss Paddington, but the neighbours don't know that and I'm trying to impress them."

"I imagine old Mrs Stockworth across the way is impressed enough by now. Come inside, James, before the tea gets cold."

Hudson slammed the bonnet down, turned off the Bentley's engine, waved towards Mrs Stockworth's dark silent villa and followed Miss Paddington inside.

"But you're right, Miss Paddington," he said, walking into the kitchen. "I should get something a little faster. Let the Bentley have a break now and then. Can't you just see me, driving around the

English countryside at 150 mph in a brand new sports car. On official business, of course," he added.
"I see you dead, James, if you drive around the English countryside at such speeds. Dead or in hospital. Will you have a biscuit?"

Übung 3: Welches Wort ist das „schwarze Schaf"? Unterstreichen Sie das nicht in die Reihe passende Wort!

ÜBUNG 3

1. rare, uncommon, unusual, unknown
2. surprise, overwhelm, amazon, amaze
3. impression, break, pause, interruption
4. honour, respect, glory, value
5. engine, machine, motor, mentor

"They're cowards, Mal. They're afraid of really being successful. The more successful you are, the more people watch you – and that scares them. People will look to see what A&L comes up with next."
"I'm not so sure about that, Donny."
"Well, I am. And now Jack's bringing more engineers onto the project, so that he can say it wasn't me – me and you – who did all the work. Now he'll give credit to everybody. We'll just be two names on a long list. But it's been our work the last seven or eight months, our sweat and headaches and ideas."
"Maybe they're just looking over our work to make sure we've covered everything." Evans stopped speaking a moment, looked at Award as if he were waiting for a storm and then added, "But Jack has said he's going to take me off the project soon."
"Why?"
"He said he has some other projects that need taking care of."

"What's more important than this project? He better not try to remove me from the project. This is my baby. We've got to do something to make them get this on the market quicker. And if they don't want to put it on the market, I'll find someone who will. There's a lot of competition out there."

Evans looked over at the other engineers moving around in the background. "You've got to be careful about saying such things, Donny. People will begin to take you seriously, and you might get yourself in trouble."

ernst nehmen

"I want them to take me seriously, Mal."

! ÜBUNG 4

Übung 4: Wie heißt die Formulierung auf Englisch?

1. jemanden ernst nehmen to take somebody seriously
2. sich etwas ausdenken to come up with something
3. jemandem Glauben schenken to give credit to somebody
4. jemanden von einem Projekt abziehen to take somebody of the project
5. jemanden in ein Projekt einbinden bring somebody onto a project
6. sich um etwas kümmern taking care of

An older man in a black and white pinstriped suit walked into the plant with Jack Donleavy.

"Award, come over here."

"Just a minute, sir."

Award finished with the person he'd been talking to and then walked over to the two men.

"Mr Woolcott," Donleavy said, standing between them, "this is Donald Award, the young man who developed the enhanced engine you heard about this morning."

"Donald, this is Mr Woolcott." Donleavy didn't have to say he was the CEO of A&L. Everyone knew it.

Mr Woolcott extended his arm and the two men shook hands, looking each other directly in the eye.

"How do you do?" said Woolcott.

"How do you do?" said Award.

"You have done an excellent job, lad. The improvements you and your colleagues have made on this motor could turn us into a market leader."

"My colleagues?"

"Yes," Donleavy answered quickly, "the senior engineers –"

"It's my work," Award interrupted. "Malcolm Evans and I are the ones who did all the work, developing and testing it. The last few weeks, the senior engineers have only been running the tests Mal and I already ran successfully – months ago, I would add."

"You can't be too safe," said Woolcott.

"I understand," said Award. "But at the very least we should be doing different tests. They're wasting their time running the same tests that we did four months ago."

"You can't be too safe," Woolcott repeated.

"I beg to differ, sir. With all due respect, you can be too safe. At any other sports car company, this project would be much farther along."

"We're behind this project," Woolcott answered, suddenly looking angry, "we're behind it one hundred percent."

"This project is ahead of you," Award responded, "well ahead of you, both of you," and walked away from his boss and the A&L CEO.

ÜBUNG 5 !

Übung 5: Welche Wörter gehören zu welchem Bereich? Ordnen Sie die Substantive in Klammern richtig zu!
(a) lad, b) engine, c) CEO, d) development, e) colleagues, f) market leader, g) project, h) chap, j) success, k) coward, l) competition, m) innovation, n) bonnet)

1. Technik b d g m n
2. Geschäftswelt c f j l e g
3. persönlicher Umgang a ~~g~~ h k

Later that day, Award walked into Donleavy's office in a rage.
"Why wasn't I in that meeting? I'm the one who had the ideas. I'm the one who has done all the work. I know more about this than anybody else. This is my project, and I should be the one representing it."
"At any other company you'd have been fired for the way you spoke to Woolcott this afternoon."
"At any other company, I'd have met Woolcott this morning and described my project to him. At any other company, the meeting this morning would have been held months ago."
"I'm the director of Research and Development, Donny. I make the decisions."
"I deserve credit for the work I've done. At the very least, I want a pay rise. Mr Woolcott knows what this means to A&L or he wouldn't have come down here."
"I'll have to get back to you about the pay rise, but I'd advise you to remember your place here, Donny."
"I know my place here, Jack. I'm the best engineer in R&D. And if you don't want to treat me like that, then I can go somewhere else. Should I give you a list of all of A&L's competitors?"

"Don't threaten me," Donleavy said.
"I'm just telling you, all the ideas are up here," he tapped his head with his finger. "They're all up there." Award turned around and left the office, walking to his own office.

*Übung 6: Setzen Sie die passenden Formen von **advise** in die entsprechenden Lücken ein!*
(advisory, advise, advisable, advice, advised, adviser)

1. I would advise you to remember Mr Woolcott's words.
2. He is my mentor and my professional adviser.
3. It is not advisable to talk to a CEO in that way!
4. He acts in a purely advisory function.
5. He was poorly advised.
6. I don't need your advice!

"Production and Quality Control," said a female voice.
"This is Jack, may I speak to Marv?", asked Donleavy, referring to Marvin Good, A&L vice president.
"He's not in his office at the moment, Mr Donleavy. Can I get him to call you back?"
"Could I leave a message?"
"Certainly. Just a moment while I get a pen. Okay."
"Tell him that Donald Award has asked for a rise and that I'd suggest we give it to him to keep him here."
"Okay, I'll tell him."
"Thank you."

ÜBUNG 7

Übung 7: Wie heißen die Wörter auf Englisch?

1. Vorstandsvorsitzender CEO chief executive officer
2. Ingenieur engineer
3. Chefingenieur senior-engineer
4. Forschungs- und Entwicklungsleiter Head of Research & Development
5. Rennfahrer racing driver

"Judging by the first sentence, this is just the thing for you, James," Miss Paddington folded the newspaper so he could read the article. Hudson and Miss Paddington were eating breakfast together. "Some awful English sports car company has just developed a new engine that can go as fast as those awful Italian cars."

"You're right, Miss Paddington, that is just the thing for me."

"You can live out your death wish, though you really are a bit too old for one."

"You're as young as you feel, Miss Paddington."

"I don't want to hear any of that American nonsense," she said. "You were over there far too long and you came back full of …"

"You're quite right."

Hudson read through the brief article and then handed it back to Miss Paddington.

"That was quick," she said, setting the paper on the table.

"There wasn't much to it. A&L, one of the better sports car manufacturers, has a new engine. We don't know what's new about it or when it's going to be on the market. All we know is it exists."

"That's not news, James, that's advertising."

"I quite agree, Miss Paddington, but it is good advertising."

Übung 8: Setzen Sie die verschiedenen Formen von ***advertise*** *ein!*
(advert, advertised, advertisement, advertiser, advertising)

1. He is the head of an ____________ agency.
2. This company never was a big ____________.
3. He placed an ____________ in yesterday's newspapers.
4. He is a good ____________ for his company.
5. He ____________ his colleague as the best young engineer in the company.

The phone rang.
"Jack Donleavy."
"Jack, this is Marv. I would like to know how this article on the new engine got in the newspaper."
"I'd like to know myself. I'm holding a meeting this morning to find out. I'm going to ask everyone, starting with Award."
"Someone leaked that information, and it's going to put pressure on us. Woolcott rang me a little while ago. He was very displeased. Some of the other companies haven't had a new idea in years, and they may start trying to get information on this new engine. Others will finally be inspired to wake up and try something new. You asked me about giving Award a rise. Find out what he knows about the newspaper article first and then decide about the pay rise. I'd suggest moving him up two pay levels. His work is first rate, even if he isn't. But I'll be very upset with you if he's the source. I'll hold you responsible. You've got to keep your employees happy, Jack. If you can't do it, we'll have to find someone who can."
"I'll do my best, Marv, but Award is difficult. Anything else?"
"That's it for now, Jack. Goodbye."

"Bye."

Donleavy hung up the phone and yelled out into the hallway. "Meeting in fifteen minutes!"

ÜBUNG 9 !

Übung 9: Fügen Sie jeweils die richtige Präposition bzw. Konjunktion ein!

(about, on, to, that, between, for, against)

1. He decided ____________ himself to demand a pay rise.
2. The rise which has been decided ____________ is really high.
3. Donleavy decided ____________ a meeting should be held.
4. Donleavy decided ____________ ask his people about the newspaper article.
5. They had to decide ____________ two alternatives.
6. Award hoped that his boss wouldn't decide ____________ a rise.
7. Woolcott has to decide ____________ tomorrow.

All the engineers were sitting in their chairs when Donleavy entered the meeting room, carrying the newspaper. He glanced over at Award, who was looking at his fingers. Donleavy opened the newspaper and held it up.

"Anybody know anything about this?"

"I read it already," one engineer offered.

"Good publicity," said another.

"It isn't good publicity," Donleavy countered, "because we didn't approve it. We have a publications office that manages all press releases. They know nothing about this."

"I expect they'd better start keeping up with developments in the company," Award said.
Some of the other engineers laughed.

Übung 10: Setzen Sie die Wörter in Klammern in die Lücken ein!
(competition, matter, permission, designing, consequences, avoided)

"This isn't a laughing 1. ___matter___. Woolcott isn't amused and I'm not amused either. Does anyone here have anything to confess?" Donleavy looked around the room, at each engineer, but looked longest at Award, who 2. ___avoided___ his glance.

"Anyone have *anything* to confess, *Award*?"

"I confess that I am responsible for 3. ___designing___ a new engine that's going to put A&L back in 4. ___competition___."

"I'm not talking about the new engine, Donny; I'm talking about the newspaper article. Did you speak to a journalist about the new engine – without company 5. ___permission___?"

"I spoke to no one," Award answered, a curious emphasis on the word 'spoke'.

"And you, Evans, did you speak to anyone?"

"I don't even talk to my girlfriend about it, Jack. Maybe it was Woolcott. He loves to talk."

"That's enough out of you, Mal. So no one here spoke to a journalist, no one gave out any information on the new engine? Now's the time to speak up. Later, it'll be too late and there will be 6. __________."

"Come off it, Jack," Award said. "Whoever spoke to the newspaper did A&L a favour. Maybe now, the company will finally decide to do something with this new engine. We'll be old men by the time A&L decides it's run enough tests. Look at Scott over there," Award said, pointing at a bald-headed man opposite him. "He had a full head of hair when we started these tests."
Everyone in the meeting laughed except for Donleavy.
"This isn't funny, lads. Woolcott, the board of directors, myself and others, we make the decisions, not you Award, not you Evans, not any of the rest of you. There will be disciplinary action if we find out who is responsible for this leak. Meeting over."

Jack Donleavy was in his office, sitting at his desk, holding the phone several inches away from his ear.
"Donleavy, if you can't keep your people under control, we'll find someone else to head R&D, do you hear me?"
"Yes, but Mr Woolcott, I can't watch them twenty-four hours a day."
"I don't want to hear what you can't do, Donleavy. I want to hear what you are going to do."

"He denies everything, Mr Woolcott."
"Award?"
"Yes."
"I am holding you responsible. These are your people. If you can't keep them quiet, then we'll find someone who can."

"I'd like to see you find someone who can keep this group of misfits happy and productive, Mr Woolcott. Besides, it's your refusal to allow the engine to move onto the next stage of testing that has everyone frustrated," and with that, Donleavy slammed the phone down. He stood up from his desk and walked out into the workshop.

Übung 11: Spiegelt der Satz den richtigen Sachverhalt wider? Markieren Sie mit richtig ✔ oder falsch – !

1. Jack Donleavy is the director of Research and Development at A&L.
2. A&L is a minor sports car manufacturer.
3. An article on the new engine from A&L was in the newspaper.
4. Donleavy was suspected of having given information to a journalist.
5. Mr Woolcott was very angry about the newspaper article.
6. Woolcott put pressure on Donleavy to find the person responsible for the leak.
7. Award finally admitted to giving information to the newspaper.

Hudson was at his desk filling in forms when the phone rang.
"Hudson, come in here please, I want you."
"Yes, Sir Reginald," he said, and put the phone down.
It had been a busy morning for Hudson. He had a huge pile of paperwork to catch up on. The call from Sir Reginald, however, came at just the right moment.

A minute later, Hudson walked into his boss's office. Sir Reginald was one of the people at Scotland Yard who made 'the big decisions', as he was fond of saying. Hudson immediately sat across from the older man, without being invited.

ÜBUNG 12 !

Übung 12: Übersetzen Sie!

1. Donleavy berichtete Mr Woolcott, dass Award alles abstritt.

____

____

2. Woolcott verlangte von Donleavy, seine Leute unter Kontrolle zu haben.

____

____

3. Er drohte ihm, einen anderen Leiter für die Forschungs- und Entwicklungsabteilung zu finden.

____

____

4. Nach dem Telefonat ging er wütend zu seinen Leuten in die Werkstatt.

____

____

5. Hudson hasste es, Formulare auszufüllen.

____

____

6. Er hatte an diesem Morgen viel Schreibarbeiten zu erledigen.

____

____

"Tea?" Sir Reginald offered.
"No, thank you."
"Coffee?"
"No, thank you."
"Well, it's too early for a martini, so we'll just get straight to business then. A young man named Donald Award has turned up missing."
"That's a job for the police."
"Yes, it would be if he were a teenager having difficulties with his parents."
"Jenny giving you problems, Sir Reginald?" Hudson laughed, referring to Sir Reginald's granddaughter, who had just turned thirteen.
"Can I continue, Hudson? This is not a teenager, and it's not my granddaughter. This is an engineer for A&L Sports Cars. He recently – a little less than a year ago – designed a new kind of engine. He's been gone a week now."

Übung 13: Formen Sie die Sätze in die indirekte Rede um!

1. "Well it's too early for a martini," Sir Reginald said.

   Sir Reginald said that it was too early for a martini.

2. “A young man has turned up missing,” Sir Reginald reported.

SR reported that a young man had turned up missing

3. “Is Jennifer giving you problems?” Hudson asked.

H asked if Jennifer was giving him problems

4. “Can I continue?” asked Sir Reginald.

SR asked if he could continued

5. “The young man has been gone a week now,” Sir Reginald said.

SR said that the young man had been gone a week now.

“A missing person?”

“Until this morning. Look at this.” Sir Reginald passed a plain white piece of paper across the desk to Hudson. On the paper was written a very simple message, ‘We have him’. The handwriting was as plain as the note – no ornamentation, just small, square letters.

“Written by an engineer,” Hudson hypothesized.

“Perhaps. A&L’s CEO, Mr Martin Woolcott, fears that the kidnapping is actually an act of corporate espionage. Someone is out to get the design for their new engine. Sports car enthusiasts are quite willing to pay large sums of money for their cars.”

“Have the parents been notified?”

“The mother’s dead and the father’s whereabouts are unknown. Your job, first and foremost, is naturally to get the lad back safely. But you must also find out why he has been taken and who, if anyone, hired the kidnappers. No doubt the ransom, when one is finally demanded, will only be a deception.”

ÜBUNG 14

Übung 14: Wie heißen die Wörter auf Englisch?

1. Firmenspionage corporate espionage
2. Druckbuchstaben square letters
3. Entführung kidnapping
4. Motor engine
5. Lösegeld randsom
6. Täuschung deception

"I'm not sure I'd say 'no doubt', Sir Reginald. He's valuable to A&L too. They'll be very happy to have their star engineer back, I should think. Goose and the golden egg and all that."
"Trust me, Hudson, this is going to be far more complicated than it looks at first glance. But I doubt Mr Award is in great danger."
"Who was the letter addressed to?"
"Woolcott – the CEO – got it, but there was no addressee. A vagabond attempted to enter the building. Naturally, the security guard on duty removed him immediately. There was a bit of a struggle, but he got the vagrant out. Only afterwards did he notice the letter on the lobby floor. Naturally, everyone had heard that Award was missing and could put one plus one together."

ÜBUNG 15

Übung 15: Setzen Sie die Sätze ins Passiv!

1. They sent back the letter to the addressee.
The letter was send back to the addressee

2. The security guard removed the vagabond.

The vagabound was removed by the s. g

3. The vagrant surprised the security guard.

The s.g. was surprised by the vagrant.

4. The guard noticed the letter on the lobby floor.

The leter on the lobby floor was noticed by the g.

5. Sports car enthusiasts pay large sums for their cars.

Large sums for their cars are paid. by sports car entusiasts.

"That delivery couldn't have worked better. It probably wasn't even a real vagabond."
"Perhaps not, but that won't help us at the moment. We're dealing with the automotive industry, not London West End theatre. I'd suggest you pay a visit to A&L immediately."
"Will do."
"Remember, Hudson, these corporate crimes always go deep. I have a feeling about this one."
Hudson walked back to his office, cleared his desk of his half-finished work and left the building.

He walked into the A&L office near the outskirts of London. The main building was six storeys tall and behind it was a fenced-in area where the engineers worked on their projects.
At the reception, he showed his badge and asked for directions to Mr Woolcott's office.
The lift took him to the top storey.

"I'd like to see Mr Woolcott, please," he said, showing his badge. "Tell him Inspector Hudson from Scotland Yard is here."

Übung 16: Setzen Sie die Übersetzung der Wörter in Klammern in die Lücken!
(führte, ziemlich, irgendwie, Ingenieur, Vergangenheitsform, entführt, kürzlich, Grund)

ÜBUNG 16 !

"Inspector Hudson, I'm Martin Woolcott. Please come with me."

Woolcott 1. ____________________ Hudson into his office. "Please have a seat, Inspector," he said, pointing towards a chair and moving around behind his desk and sitting. "You got here 2. ________________ quickly."

"Well, it was either that or do more paperwork," Hudson said with a smile.

"So they keep you in paperwork too."

"The government requires everything in triplicate."

"The government doesn't require that I make a profit, but they do require that I pay my rates."

"Right," said Hudson. "You have an 3. ________________ who is missing and now appears to have been 4.________________."

"Not just any engineer, Inspector, but a very important one. Donald Award. You may have seen a report of a new engine in the newspaper 5. ______________?"

"Yes, I saw it."

"That's his baby. We had high hopes for him."

"Why, 'we had high hopes for him'? Do you have any 6. ______ ______ for speaking of him in the 7. ______________?"

"No, we hope to 8. ______________ get him safely back."

"Do you have any idea who might have kidnapped him?"
"No. Look at our competition. Any of them might have done it. We're in a very competitive branch of the automotive industry. There haven't been many significant developments in the last few years. Award's work was about to change all that."
"It is about to change all that," Hudson insisted.
"Quite right."
"Can you tell me how long he has been missing?"
"He didn't show up for work last Friday and he's not been here since."
"And today's Thursday. So he was probably taken a week ago. Why did you hesitate to call?"
"Quite frankly, we thought he was hiding out at home because he was angry with his boss, Jack Donleavy. Donleavy thought that he might have taken time off from work without letting anyone know. A couple of years ago he took a week off without telling anyone. He went to Ibiza and came back with a nice tan. Donleavy naturally threatened to sack him but didn't. Instead, he cut his year-end bonus in half. I understand Award took his colleagues out for a night on the town with what remained."
"So this time, no one went by his flat to see if he answered?"
"I believe Donleavy might have, but you'd have to ask him."

Übung 17: Bringen Sie die Fragesätze in die richtige Reihenfolge!

1. have who him might idea kidnapped anybody have an does?

Does anybody ~~might~~ have an idea who might have kidnapped him?

2. Mr how has Woolcott missing know long been does Award?

Does M W know how long Award has been missing

3. did to the why call hesitate you police?

Why did you hesitate to call the police

4. without ever taken anybody off has time Award telling?

as Award ever ~~has~~ taken off time without ~~ever~~ telling anybody

5. by flat go see home he anybody was did his to if?

Did anybody

6. past all time speak Award in you the of tense why do the?

Why do you speak all the time in past tense of Award?

Woolcott led Hudson to the lift. They were going to meet Award's boss and his colleagues. While waiting for the lift, Woolcott's administrative assistant passed by.

"Are you busy right now, Madeline?"

"I'm always busy, Mr Woolcott," she said with a weary smile.

"Okay, not a fair question. Would you take Inspector Hudson down to Donleavy's office and show him around. He's here to help us with Award's disappearance. Is that okay with you?" he asked Hudson.

"I'll stop by before I leave," Hudson said.
"Please do," Woolcott responded and walked back towards his office.

ÜBUNG 18

Übung 18: Setzen Sie die in Klammern stehenden Wendungen in die entsprechenden Lücken ein!
(showed … around, on show, nothing to show, shown up, took on, took over, take … down)

1. The brand new sports car is ____________ in the exhibition room.
2. Has Mr Hudson ____________ yet?
3. They ____________ the new colleague ____________ the company.
4. Would you please ____________ Mr Hudson ____________ to the ground floor?
5. We haven't got any new results. There's ____________.
6. There was too much work for us alone so the boss ____________ a new employee.
7. The former CEO is not in charge any longer. Another person ____________.

They stepped into the lift.
"I'm James Hudson," he said.
"Madeline Jones."
An attractive, dark-haired woman in her mid-thirties, she stared at

the floor the whole time they were in the lift. The door opened, and she jumped out like a horse out of the starting gates. Hudson had to almost run to keep up. She led him into another building, turned several corners and led him down a long hallway.
"Do you always walk so fast, Ms Jones, or is this a race?"
"This is Jack Donleavy's office. He's director of Research and Development. His secretary should be able to help you locate Mr Donleavy." That said, she vanished.

Übung 19: Unterstreichen Sie die englische Entsprechung der folgenden Substantive im Text!
(1. Faxgerät, 2. Drucker, 3. Aktenschränke, 4. Schreibmaschine, 5. Bereich, 6. Sekretärin)

Hudson knocked on the door and entered as he was bidden.
"I'm Inspector Hudson, Scotland Yard," he said to a red-haired woman in her forties. The office was filled with filing cabinets, a computer, printer, fax machine and even an old typewriter. "I'd like to speak with Mr Donleavy."
"I'll take you to him," she volunteered. "How'd you get here?" Hudson explained. "I suppose some people are scared of Scotland Yard inspectors," she said, attempting to explain Jones' behaviour.
"Unfortunately, it's always the wrong people who are afraid of us," Hudson said with a smile. "I wish the tall men weighing in at 14 stone were scared of me. They take rather more convincing."
They walked a short distance into a large open warehouse-like area.

"Jack," she shouted.
A head lifted and a man about the same age as Inspector Hudson, though looking ten years older, started walking over to them.

"The Inspector is here to see you, Mr Donleavy."
"Inspector Hudson, Scotland Yard," he said, introducing himself.
"Jack Donleavy. You're here about Donny Award."
"Exactly. He worked with everyone here?"
"Yes. But he worked closest with Malcolm Evans. The others co-operated with him, but he wasn't always easy to work with."
Donleavy took Hudson around and introduced him to all of Award's colleagues. When he was introduced to Evans, Hudson told him that he would want to speak to him later.
"I'll do anything I can to help," Evans answered.

ÜBUNG 20

Übung 20: Bringen Sie die Buchstaben in die richtige Reihenfolge und bilden Sie sinnvolle Wörter!

1. sollageuce ____collegiaes____
2. dortniceu ____________
3. petttam ____attempt____
4. nexlaip ____explain____
5. varouhebi ____________
6. gininvoncc ____________

Walking back to Donleavy's office, Hudson asked about suspects.
"Perhaps one of the other sports car producers, after reading the article in the newspaper last week. That wouldn't surprise me. He also has a mouth on him."
"What do you mean?"
"Award can be direct to the point of rudeness. He is brilliant but quite aware of it. Sometimes, he could annoy others around him."

"Enough to kidnap him?"

"No. There has never even been a fight. His colleagues know he's brilliant. Besides, he isn't just arrogant; he can also be quite decent too. But he does know his worth, and he isn't shy about trumpeting it from the mountaintops."

"Not an easy person then."

"Not at all. When he wants something, he pushes until he gets his way or until he finally gives up. Usually, he gets what he wants."

"So, why did you suggest that his mouth might get him into trouble?"

"If he met with representatives from another company and didn't like what they had to say to him, he might have said the wrong thing to the wrong person. That wouldn't surprise me one bit."

Übung 21: Vervollständigen Sie die Sätze mit den passenden Formulierungen in Klammern!

(to the point of, at the point of, to have a point, to make a point of, point of view, to point out, at the point of no return)

1. He understood her argumentation because she had a point.
2. He was at the point of leaving this company.
3. He pointed out that Donald Award could be very rude.
4. We have to continue this venture. There's no way back. We're at the point of no return
5. He is honest ________________ cruelty.

6. Award ____________________ being direct to other people.

7. From Donleavy's ____________________, nobody at A&L kidnapped Award.

Hudson asked Donleavy about the last time he had seen Award and whether he had tried to find Award during his absence.
"I called his home several times and even sent Evans by, but no luck. Now we know why."
"Where is his office?"
Donleavy led Hudson to the office Award shared with Evans and three other engineers, leading him to Award's computer.
Hudson leaned down and turned the computer on.
"I'm afraid you're not going to be able to look at Award's files. They're secret."
"Not anymore. They might help tell us who kidnapped him or why."
"You're going to have to speak to someone in the IT Department if you want to look at Award's files."
Hudson picked up the phone on Award's desk and handed it to Donleavy. "Please ring Woolcott. I'm not playing games. Have him call IT and they can call me with all the codes I need."

ÜBUNG 22 !

Übung 22: Setzen Sie die passenden Substantive in die entsprechenden Lücken ein!
(programs, emails, requests, extension, directories, letters, items, projects)

"If you need me for anything," Donleavy said, leaving the engineers' office, "my 1. __extension__ is 4117."

Hudson scrolled down the list of 2. _directories_ on Award's computer. He saw the computer 3. _programmes_ Award used when designing. He looked through Award's documents directory and found 4. _letters_ he'd written to various companies around the UK and abroad, but nothing unusual. The letters were 5. _requests_ for machinery or parts or other 6. _items_ that he needed for his various 7. _projects_. Hudson glanced through Award's 8. _email_. He had over a thousand of them, dating back nearly a year.

The phone rang at Award's desk.
"Hello," Hudson said, wondering just who might be calling.
"Woolcott here. We have just had a call from the kidnappers."
"I'll be right up."
Hudson turned off the computer, put the piece of paper with Award's user names and passwords in his pocket and left.
Hudson walked into Woolcott's office. Sitting in it, in addition to Woolcott, were Donleavy and Marvin Good. Good stood and introduced himself.
"So, what happened?" Hudson asked.
"They told us they have Award and that he's safe," said Woolcott.
"Did they say who they were or what they wanted?"
"No, they didn't even mention how much money they were going to demand. It was a very brief call."
"Tell me exactly what the caller said," Hudson requested.
Woolcott said, "He said, "We have Donald Award. We'll call tomorrow at 3 pm to tell you our demands." Then he hung up.

"Was he at a payphone? Could you hear cars or other people?"

"I – I don't know," he said. "It all happened so quickly."

"You have to learn to listen for these things. It could help us find Award or even save his life. Were you alone?"

"Yes, I was. I called Donleavy and Good after I spoke with you."

Hudson walked to the secretary. "Did you put the caller through?"

"He said he had important information about Donald Award, so I thought it best to …."

"You did exactly what you should have, Ms –"

"– Jagger, Kathleen Jagger."

"You did fine, Ms Jagger. Did you happen to notice anything in the background during the phone call?"

"No, it was too short. I connected the call to Mr Woolcott as quickly as I could."

"Tomorrow, we'll do things a little differently," Hudson said and walked back into Woolcott's office. "We'll be here tomorrow at 3 pm. Do you have a speaker phone, so we can all listen in?"

"Yes, I do."

"Good."

Donleavy and Good left the office.

ÜBUNG 23 !

Übung 23: Übersetzen Sie!

1. Sie können mich jederzeit anrufen. Meine Durchwahl ist 6478.

You can call me every time. My extension is 647?

2. Hudson sah auf Awards Computer alle Ordner und Dateien durch.

Hudson looked at all directions and programs which are on Awards computer

3. Martin Good stellte sich Hudson vor.

MG introdicing himself to Hudson

4. Wie viel Geld fordern die Entführer?

How much money the kidnepped wanted?

5. Es war nur ein kurzes Gespräch.

It was a short call

6. Ms Jagger stellte den Anrufer durch.

MJ ~~co~~ connected the caller

"Where are you going now, Inspector Hudson?" Woolcott asked.
"I'm going back to Award's office to look around some more."
"So you were not finished? Can you find your way back there?"
"I believe so. Do you know if Award had any enemies here at A&L?"
"I only met the lad for the first time last week. I know that he and Donleavy banged heads regularly, but I don't think that made them enemies. Such relationships can be positive."
"Thank you."

Hudson returned to Award's office. He turned on the computer and then walked around the office. On another desk he saw a picture of two young men sitting on tiered seats at a football match. One of the men had a dark complexion and was smiling broadly; the other had blond hair and was making a silly face for the camera. Just then, Malcolm Evans walked in.
"Hello, Evans." Hudson said.
"Hello, Inspector."
Hudson asked if the blond-haired young man was Award.

"Yes, that's Donny."

"You're friends?"

"Yes."

"Did Donny have any enemies?"

"No. Well, anyone who got in his way was an enemy of sorts. But Donny didn't hold grudges. And I don't think anyone else, besides maybe Donleavy, was mad at him for long."

Groll hegen

ÜBUNG 24

Übung 24: Machen Sie aus zwei Sätzen einen! Verwenden Sie eine Konjunktion oder das Gerundium!

1. Hudson saw a picture of two men. They sat on tiered seats at a football match.

   Hudson saw a picture of two men sitting on tiered seats at a football match.

2. Hudson picked up the phone on Awards desk. He handed it to Donleavy.

   H picked up the phone on A desk handing it to D

3. Woolcott sat in his office. He was waiting for a call.

   W sat in his office waiting for a call

4. Hudson went back to Award's office. He held a cup of coffee in his hand.

   H went back to A office holding a cup of coffee in his hand

5. The man waved his hand. He was making a funny face into the camera.

The man waved his hand making a funny face into the camera

6. Malcolm Evans walked in. He greeted Hudson.

ME walked in greeting Hudson

"Donleavy?"

"Yes, Donny is always pushing Donleavy, trying to get things through faster. And Donleavy always tries to slow things down. Donny could sometimes really push hard, though. And Donleavy thinks Donny leaked the news of the new engine, which he probably did. Donny isn't easy to work with, sometimes, but really he's all right. I wouldn't want to be his boss though."

Hudson sat in Award's office in front of his computer and began going through emails. He found nothing of interest, however. There were communications with suppliers where Award complained of slow deliveries:

Dear Sir,

I placed an order on 15 February for part number 13256A and have yet to receive the part.

While I recognize that international shipping requires longer delivery times, I made it clear when ordering that the shipment should be a 'rush shipment' and that any extra costs incurred should be charged to A&L.

Please check to see when or if the part was shipped. A&L, however, will not pay any special shipping charges, since the shipment was neither 'rush' nor 'express'. I imagine, in fact, that it has been shipped by rowing boat.

Yours faithfully,

Donald Award
Engineer, R&D

Übung 25: Vervollständigen Sie die Wortverbindungen!

1. to slow things ________________ (verlangsamen)
2. to push ________________ (Druck ausüben)
3. to know ________________ certain (sicher sein)
4. to place ________________ an order (eine Bestellung aufgeben)
5. express delivery ________________ (Expressversand)
6. long delivery times ________________ (lange Lieferzeiten)

Hudson found similar letters, but nothing that would lead to kidnapping. Award seemed to enjoy being in the right.
"Mr Evans, can you take me to Award's flat?"
"I can take you there, but I can't get you in."
"Does his landlord or landlady live in the same building?"
"Yes, his landlady lives on the first floor."

Hudson followed Evans to the building where Award had until recently lived. It was an old building in Camden. The landlady was unfriendly and suspicious but when Hudson finally convinced her that he really was from Scotland Yard and that Donald Award had done nothing wrong, she at last gave him a key to Award's flat.

Hudson and Evans went up the stairs to the flat. The air inside was stale. Clearly, no one had been there in days.

"It just struck me," Hudson said to Evans, "but we don't even know where Award was when he was kidnapped." Hudson glanced around the flat, but there were no chairs or tables on their sides. "It doesn't look like there was any struggle here. He must have been taken on the street. Someone knew where he usually went and picked him up on the street."

Übung 26: Setzen Sie die Präpositionen ein!
(next to, around, into, on, for, under, to, of, from, in)

"Or 1. __in__ a pub. Donny always went 2. __into__ a pub after work 3. __for__ a pint or two. He wasn't a heavy drinker, but he always had a pint or two after work."

Hudson wandered around the flat. There was a large living room and a bedroom and a small kitchen. The stereo equipment and the television were all relatively new.

"Always the best for Mr Award," Hudson said.

"Work hard, play hard," Evans responded.

"So where is his computer? I assume he has one at home."

Evans looked 4. ________ the living room and then quickly walked 5. ________ the bedroom.

"That's strange. He had a laptop for home, but it's gone."

"Whoever has Award must have used his key to get in. Where did he usually have the computer?" Evans pointed to a small wooden table, 6. ________ the shelves with his stereo system.

Under the table was a rubbish bin filled with paper. Hudson pulled it out and set it on the table. He began removing sheets of paper from the bin and spreading them out on the table. What he found were versions of a letter with ink corrections on them. Award had been working on a letter to A&L's competitors, though since he had apparently been planning on doing a mail merge, the space where the mailing address would have been was taken up with codes.

"This is an old-fashioned way to work," Hudson said. "You can do corrections on the computer. You can use 'preview' to see what the document is going to look like before printing it."

"Donny liked to see what the finished product was going to look like, so he often printed things up. That drove Donleavy mad, the waste of paper. But that was Donny; he always had to do things his way."

Hudson read:

Dear Sirs,

I have worked at A&L now for seven years. I recently developed a new kind of engine that will allow sports cars to attain speeds of up to 200 mph. You read about it in the newspaper, and it is true.

A&L, unfortunately, do not see the value in the project. Your company, however, may have more foresight. If you are interested in offering me a position and providing an atmosphere where I can further develop my ideas, please call me on my mobile phone on 0776 40087.

I look forward to hearing from you.

Übung 27: Setzen Sie die Sätze ins Passiv!

1. Engineers constantly develop new ideas.

Engineers ~~had~~ had constantly developed new ideas

2. The company provided a creative atmosphere.

The company has provided a creative atmosphere

3. A&L offered him a new position.

A&L had offered him a new position

4. A&L didn't value Award's ambitious project.

5. You can do corrections easier with a computer than with a typewriter.

"It appears your friend was looking for employment at other sports car manufacturers."

"That wouldn't surprise me. A&L hasn't really been giving him the support he thinks he deserves."
"And what do you think?"
"I think they supported him, but not as much as the project deserved. They put up roadblocks to our work. We had to redo tests we'd already done many times. I'm not sure why they wanted to delay the project, but Donny felt sure that they did."
"Why would they delay the project? What benefit could there be?"
"Donny thought it was simply Donleavy's revenge. But I've seen other projects move faster. I don't know why Donleavy would slow the project."
"Those two didn't get on, eh?"
"They got on all right, but Donleavy never seemed very enthusiastic about this project."
"You didn't plan on leaving London any time soon, did you?"
"No sir, why?"
"I may need your help, Mr Evans."
"You may call me Mal."
"You may call me Inspector Hudson."
Hudson took down the young man's address and phone number.

ÜBUNG 28 !

Übung 28: Unterstreichen Sie die richtige Alternative!

Outside (1.) in/at the street with Evans, Hudson asked where Award went for his two daily pints of bitter.
"We always went to the Vickie, just around the corner from here."
"You live (2.) around/about here?"
Evans pointed (3.) over/across the street at another building.
"Let's go. I'll get us a round," Hudson said.
They walked a short distance, turned a corner, and there was a dark

wooden façade with *Victoria Pub and Victuals* written across a window. They entered. The pub was busy with men and women drinking their first pint after (4.) job/work.

Hudson pushed his way up to the bar.

"Come with me, Evans," he said.

At the bar, Hudson ordered two pints. While waiting for them, he asked (5.) whether/weather Evans recognised the barman.

"Yes. He knows me."

The two beers came and Hudson gave the barman a ten pound note. "Can you tell me the last time you saw Donny Award?" he asked.

The barman glanced at Evans before (6.) repeating/answering.

"Sometime last week."

"Was he here alone?"

The man thought a moment, again looking at Evans before answering. "He came in alone and left with three men."

"Did they look like (7.) vagrants/businessmen?"

"No. They didn't stand (8.) out/in. All I remember was hearing them talk about a new engine he had developed. He's been coming here (9.) for/since years, and I never knew he was a whiz kid. Imagine that."

At home that night, sitting in his study drinking a glass of sherry, Hudson began thinking about his day. It had taken a sharp turn for the worse when Sir Reginald called. Hudson did not like dealing with kidnappings. He'd seen too many turn bloody, the hostage ending up dead and the ransom money gone. "I wonder if he sent any letters out? Did he actually finish his letter and post it to any other sports car manufacturers? Sir Reginald thought this would be a complicated case, which makes me think that the place to look is inside A&L, but we'll see what happens tomorrow and the hostage-takers demands."

The next morning, Friday, Hudson stopped by Scotland Yard to see if he had any mail. There were requests for the paperwork he had abandoned the previous day, but nothing of any importance, by Hudson's standards at any rate. Sir Reginald was in a meeting. Therefore, Hudson drove on to A&L. Before he got into his car, however, he called Mr Woolcott on his mobile phone.

"Woolcott speaking."

"Hello Mr Woolcott, this is Inspector Hudson. I'm on my way over and plan to continue my research there."

"By all means."

"Actually, I'm going to see Donleavy first and then do a little more research in the R&D department. Can you tell me any other departments that might be of interest to me? Maybe just give me a brief overview of A&L."

"Of course."

"Thank you, Mr Woolcott."

ÜBUNG 29 !

Übung 29: Setzen Sie die Wendungen in Klammern in die entsprechenden Lücken ein!
(at all means, by no means, by means of, beyond … means, within … means)

1. Our company cannot afford new investments. They are __________ our __________.
2. ______________ looking through Award's files, Hudson hoped to find out something new.
3. A&L ______________ wanted to have the public informed about the new engine.

4. Hudson wanted to continue his research in the R&D department

_______________.

5. A&L financed all of Award's projects. They were __________ the company's __________.

"We've got Sales & Marketing, Accounts, IT, Personnel, Public Relations, Manufacturing, Research & Development and Quality Control. They're all fairly isolated from one another. I doubt that Award had much contact with engineers in Manufacturing. Donleavy and a senior engineer, who serves as his assistant, are the coordinators, a sort of bridge between the two sets of engineers. You'd have to ask Donleavy if there was regular contact between Award and other departments within A&L."

"Thanks for your help."

"Thank you, Inspector. And you'll be here at 3 pm?"

"I'll be there before 3 pm."

"See you then."

Übung 30: Welche Abteilung von A&L ist gemeint? Setzen Sie den richtigen Abteilungsnamen ein!

1. The department that is concerned with the development of information technology is called IT.

2. The department that advertises and sells the sports cars is called Sales & Marketing.

3. The department concerned with the recruitment of employees is called Personnel.

4. The department responsible for the maintenance of a favourable public image of A&L is called Public Relations.

5. The department that keeps records of money, goods or services received or expended is called Quality Control.

"Can you direct me to Marketing and Sales, please?"
Hudson stood in the reception area of the large open lobby. A few days ago a vagabond had let a note fall in the same way as a woman, a hundred years earlier, might have let a handkerchief fall to the floor – both seeking to get someone's attention. But whose attention was this note supposed to get?
"Excuse me, which department do you want? They are two separate departments."
"The Sales Department, when I have to choose," he said, noticing that the woman opposite him was a strange beauty, with red hair and green eyes and pale skin that was a lighter shade of green than her eyes. There was something snake-like about her face.
"Second floor on the right."
"And who's in charge?"
"Janet O'Malley is the sales manager. If she's not in, then I reckon one of her sales reps can help you."

ÜBUNG 31 !

Übung 31: Übersetzen Sie!

1. Verkauf und Marketing sind zwei getrennte Abteilungen bei A&L.

Sales & marketing are two separate departments by A&L

2. Wer ist der Verantwortliche in der Abteilung Verkauf?

Who is in charge?

3. Die Sekretärin nannte Hudson den Namen der zuständigen Verkaufsleiterin.

The secretary gave Hudson the name of the ~~Sale~~ Head of Sales

4. In Janet O'Malleys Abteilung arbeiten viele Verkaufsvertreter.

5. Wenn die Verkaufsleiterin nicht da ist, kann Ihnen sicher einer ihrer Verkäufer weiterhelfen.

Hudson took the lift to the Sales offices on the second floor. There were several offices, each with desks for two sales reps, some occupied and some not.

He found O'Malley's office, the only single office, but the light was out and the office empty.

"She's in a meeting," said Madeline Jones, walking by.

Hudson watched the woman turn the corner. "Then I'll just have to speak with someone else," he decided.

"I'll be back in touch," he heard a woman say. Following the voice, Hudson came to the office of Charlotte Easter and Cliff Barnes – but judging by the voice, Mr Barnes was out.

ÜBUNG 32

Übung 32: Welches Wort bedeutet das Gegenteil? Kreuzen Sie an!

1. occupied
   a) ☒ free
   b) ☐ fixed
   c) ☐ freed

2. separate
   a) ☐ convenient
   b) ☒ concerned
   c) ☐ connected

3. favourable
   a) ☐ sad
   b) ☐ mad
   c) ☒ bad

4. public
   a) ☐ secret
   b) ☒ private
   c) ☐ intimate

5. previous
   a) ☐ following
   b) ☐ before
   c) ☒ afterwards

"I'm Inspector Hudson from Scotland Yard," he said, entering the office.

"Hello, I'm Charlotte Easter. What can I do for you?"

"I'd like some information."

"If you want to know about the missing engineer, then you've come to the wrong place. I've never met him. I had never even heard of him until yesterday when I heard that one of the engineers had been kidnapped. I hope they are able to free him soon."
"That's what I'm here for."
"I don't have him, Inspector," she said with a quick smile, "but that's nothing to joke about."
"No, I didn't think you had him, Ms Easter. Actually, I wanted to learn something about A&L's competition."
"Do you think people from one of the other companies might have kidnapped him?"
"I don't know, Ms Easter, I'm just trying to get a feel for things."
"We have competition all over the world. There are several companies here in England, you have the Italians with Ferrari and Lamborghini, there's Porsche, BMW in Germany, there's far too many companies to name – and it all depends on how you define 'competition'. Most of the major automobile manufacturers produce sports cars, but they aren't *really* our competition."

Übung 33: Setzen Sie die englische Übersetzung der Wörter in Klammern in die entsprechenden Lücken ein!
(Bedrohungen, Marktanalyse, Spezialisten, Stärken, Hersteller, Firmen, Konkurrenz)

ÜBUNG 33 !

"Let's narrow it down to British 1. ______________, perhaps even English companies. Who is your *real* competition, Ms Easter?"
"Our *real* competition? When we're feeling smug, we have no competition, Inspector Hudson. When our boss Janet O'Malley

talks to us in meetings and brings us down to earth, then every other sports car 2. ____________________, ever other automobile manufacturer in the world is our 3. ______________. The truth naturally lies somewhere in between."

"But?" Hudson said, attempting to lead Easter a bit.

"But if you do a 4. ____________________ – a SWOT analysis: 5. ________________________, weaknesses, opportunities and 6. ______________ – then you can narrow the field down considerably. There are five sports car firms, three of them are much smaller: Streak, Henley, Turner and then there's VF and Spirit Mark. All these manufacturers target their cars at collectors and 7. ______________, but they do sometimes sell outside that group. VF – Victor Franklin, or Very Fast as those who drive their cars like to say – is probably our closest competition."

"How do their cars compare?"

"Faster but not as nice looking, not as comfortable, not as dependable. Only the first characteristic is really important though. A lad can be charming without being handsome, can't he? A VF is the same way, for some sports car enthusiasts."

"What's the company like?"

"Run by a cut-throat named John Victor Franklin, grandson of the founder, and an eccentric, in the bad sense of the word."

"What do you mean?"

"He's a legend. He's notorious, notoriously choleric. For instance, a driver in a Henley once insulted the VF John Victor Franklin was driving while they were waiting for a light to turn green. The driver of the Henley rolled down his window and said something. It was probably nothing more than repartee, but Franklin pulled a wrench from under his seat, got out of his car and started smashing the Henley. He caused £4900 of damage in less than a minute. A bobby on the street stopped him and put him in jail before he could do more damage. If he hadn't been rich, I think they might have sent him to a psychiatric hospital. He went absolutely mad. Such stories only make the cars more valuable, I'm afraid. Their sales are a bit ahead of ours, but if Award's engine proves successful, we could very well overtake VF. Our cars are better looking. They have style. Much of the interior is handmade but the chassis and the engine are not, which means the car is more dependable than other sports cars and the performance is more precise. Handmade isn't everything."

Übung 34: Bringen Sie die Wörter in die richtige Reihenfolge und bilden Sie sinnvolle Fragen!

1. your manufactured VF one by cars more comfortable are than the?

___

___

2. founder who of VF the is?

Who is the founder of VF?

3. you mean what cut-throat do by?

What do you mean by cut-throat?

4. insult driver the Franklin how did of Henley Victor the?

5. VF's valuable A&L's why cars more than are?

Why are A&L's cars more valuable than VF's?

6. competitors' sales ahead of its are A&L's?

Are A&L's sales ahead of its competitors'?

"And the other company you mentioned? What was your other near competitor?"

"Spirit Mark. VF are the market leader, then there's Spirit Mark and then A&L. Spirit Mark make their sports cars by hand and very little has changed in their cars since the sixties. In fact, that's one of their selling points, that and their speed. They aren't as fast as VF. They're classics, traditional, nothing changes there. As far as sales figures go, Spirit Mark and A&L are almost neck and neck. Their sales figures are just ever so slightly higher."

"And is Spirit Mark run by a madman as well?"

"Well, it is a family business. But it's a more traditional, respectable kind of family, old aristocracy. VF was floated on the London Stock Exchange many years ago, so they're not family-owned anymore, though the family remain majority shareholders. And Franklin, the founder, was *nouveau riche*, so there is another difference."

"Where is the VF head office?"

"In St Albans."

"Just north of London. Quite an affluent area. And it's not far away at all. And Spirit Mark?"

"Ipswich."

"Thank you for your time. Do you have a business card, so I can ring you up if I have any more questions?"
She handed him her card and smiled. "Have a good day, Inspector."

Übung 35: Wie heißen die Wörter auf Englisch?

1. Aktionär shareholder
2. Firmensitz headquarter office
3. Gründer founder
4. Visitenkarte business card
5. Marktführer market leader
6. Verkaufszahlen sales figures
7. Familienunternehmen family business

Hudson walked into the engineers' office and sat at Award's computer. He turned it on and, while waiting for it to start, looked around the office. The windows looked onto the brick wall of the building opposite and onto oil-stained garages.
Hudson attempted to access Award's emails, but the computer reported that he had no emails. Hudson next looked in other directories and found that there too, much had recently been deleted.
"IT Help Desk, Melanie Cook."
"Ms Cook, I'm Inspector Hudson with Scotland Yard."
"Sure you are."
"Ms Cook, this is no joke. I'm Inspector Hudson with Scotland Yard, and I'm looking into the kidnapping of Donald Award. Have you heard anything about that?"
"Yes, of course. What can I do for you?"

“I have his user IDs and his passwords. He had a thousand emails yesterday, and today he has none.”

“Let me see,” she said, accessing Award’s account.

“They have been deleted,” she confirmed.

“By whom?”

“I don’t know.”

“Can you find out?”

“No.”

“Well, who would be able to do such a thing?”

“Mr Award.”

“Assuming that at the moment he has no access to his email account, which I think is a fair assumption, who else might be able to clear his account?

“Only someone with high-level security access.”

“For instance?”

“Only the people at the very top.”

“Someone like Jack Donleavy?”

“No, he shouldn’t have access.”

“But he might?”

“He might, I suppose, but he shouldn’t.”

“Who should?”

“Those of us in IT responsible for the network, the presidents, Mr Woolcott himself. But no one else, at least theoretically.”

“Thank you for your help.”

“Don’t mention it.”

Übung 36: Beantworten Sie die Fragen zum Text!

1. Why didn’t Inspector Hudson like Award’s office?

---

2. Why was Inspector Hudson able to check Award's emails?

3. What did Hudson find out about the emails?

All the emails were deleted.

4. Why couldn't Award have deleted his emails himself?

Because he is kidnapped

5. Who might have been able to clear Award's account?

Either someone was being very secretive, to protect A&L, or else there was somebody at A&L who didn't want him to find information on Award that might provide a motive for his kidnapping. Hudson hadn't actually counted on getting much information on Award's work computer, but the fact that someone had taken the step of deleting his files made it clear that someone thought there had been information there. It's easier to delete all the files, Hudson thought, than to search for a few 'sensitive' files. A more careful person, however, would not have emptied Award's account.

Hudson walked into Donleavy's office.
"Hello, Inspector Hudson."
"Hello, Mr Donleavy."
"How's your work going? Are you having any luck finding leads?"
"I'm making progress. I have a question. After speaking with some of the engineers, I have learned that Award felt that you were holding his project back. Is that true?"

"He might have thought it was me, but I was following Woolcott's orders. I don't know what his reasons were, but he wanted the programme to slow down. Maybe he wanted to be more careful, I don't know. He didn't explain it to me."
"Thank you for your time, Mr Donleavy."
"Any time."

ÜBUNG 37 !

Übung 37: Übersetzen Sie die Sätze, indem Sie die Wendung ***to want somebody to do something*** *benutzen!*

1. Hudson wollte, dass Charlotte Easter ihm Informationen über die Konkurrenz von A&L gibt.

____

____

2. Hudson wollte, dass Melanie Cook ihm sagt, wer Zugang zu Awards E-Mails hat.

____

____

3. Jemand wollte nicht, dass Hudson an Informationen kommt.

____

____

4. Hudson wollte, dass Donleavy seine Fragen beantwortet.

____

____

5. Woolcott wollte, dass die Entwicklung des neuen Motors verlangsamt wird.

Hudson left the R&D office and went up to Woolcott's office. His secretary reported that Woolcott was out of the office.

"That's okay," Hudson responded, "because you can answer my questions. Tell me how the company is structured, Ms Jagger."

"Well, there's a five-member board of directors and Mr Woolcott, the CEO. Then there are two presidents, one for Sales & Marketing/Finance and one for Manufacturing and Quality Control, which includes R&D. Then there are several vice presidents, one each for Sales & Marketing, R&D and Quality Control and another one for Manufacturing. Finally, there are directors for Sales, Marketing, Public Relations, Accounts, R&D, Quality Control, IT, Personnel, and several directors of Manufacturing, with different areas of responsibility."

"Quite a strict hierarchy."

"We're a traditional company, sir."

"But trying some rather novel tactics, it seems to me."

"Excuse me, sir?"

"What exactly does Madeline Jones do here?"

"That's really a good question," she said, lowering her voice. "I ask myself the same question. I think she does work that I don't have time to do. She's just young and good-looking and a man Woolcott's age enjoys having someone her age around. She fancies herself more than a secretary, she walks around very importantly, but I don't think she does anything that I couldn't do."

ÜBUNG 38 !

Übung 38: Lesen Sie weiter und unterstreichen Sie die Wörter mit denselben Bedeutungen!

(1. two times, 2. near by, 3. then, 4. identified, 5. several)

Hudson called Scotland Yard to have some kidnapping specialists sent to A&L to trace the phone call. Afterwards, he walked to Jones' office, which was close by Woolcott's, to see if she were in. Apparently, she had left with Woolcott or been sent on some other business. Hudson walked into her office, up to her phone and pressed a button to get a list of the most recent calls made. He recognized Woolcott's number and company extensions. In his notebook, he wrote down eight phone numbers that were to places outside of A&L. The phone's memory held twenty numbers, but Hudson found only two numbers she had called more than twice.

As Hudson stepped out of her office, Jones was walking down the hallway towards him.
"What were you doing in my office, Inspector?" she asked irritably.
"I needed to make a phone call, so I used your office which was dark and quiet. Is that a problem, Ms Jones?"
"No," she said, changing her voice, "of course not. I just don't like people in my office without my permission."
Looking at his watch, he said, "I have to help prepare for our phone call," and walked away.

"It's two minutes past three," Hudson said, glancing at his wristwatch. "Punctual devils." He smiled at his assistants from Scotland Yard. Hudson looked from Woolcott, to Donleavy, to Marvin Good, to John Greenwood the president of Manufacturing and Quality Control, to Madeline Jones, to Ms Jagger with a pen in her hand, ready to record the conversation in shorthand.

Übung 39: Setzen Sie die wörtliche Rede ins Simple Past!

ÜBUNG 39 !

1. "What are you doing in my office?"

What were you doing in my ofice?

2. "I am just using your phone."

I was just using your phone

3. "Your company is trying some rather novel tactics."

Your company was trying some ...

4. "I am following my boss's orders."

I was following my boss's order.

5. "I go home at seven."

I went home at seven.

6. "I think she does work that I don't have time for."

I thought she did work that I didn't have time for

At 3.14 pm, the phone finally rang.
"At last," said Woolcott softly. Following Hudson's signal, he picked the phone up on the third ring.
"Woolcott," he said.
"We have him," said a male voice over the speaker phone.
"We know you do," Woolcott answered, "now what do you want?"
"Am I on a speaker phone?" the caller asked.
Woolcott looked at Hudson questioningly. Hudson shrugged his shoulders, and then nodded his head to say yes, so Woolcott said, "Yes."
"Take me off the speaker phone."

Hudson walked up to Woolcott, pulled the phone away from his cheek, pressed the button for the speaker phone twice so that the phone went off speaker and then back on.
"Okay," Woolcott said, nervously putting the phone against his face.
"He won't tell us anything," the caller said. In the background a car went by.
"We'll pay you," Woolcott said, "just tell us what you want and make sure you don't do anything to harm him."
"Okay."
"Well," said Woolcott after a pause, "What do you want?"
"We want – £200,000 – in small notes."
"Okay." There was a pause in the conversation. "By when?"
"What?"
"When do you want the *blooming* money?"
"Monday at noon." The phone suddenly went dead.
"He didn't approve of your language, apparently," Hudson said.
"He never even said where the money was to be delivered," Greenwood said, shaking his head. "These people are obviously beginners. TV actors would have done a much better job," he added, standing up and leaving the room. "You'll have more trouble giving them the money than getting it back, Inspector Hudson."

"Did you get a location?" Hudson asked his colleagues.
"Yes, it was a payphone in Soho."
One of Hudson's associates phoned the location in to colleagues waiting in a car and then they left Woolcott's office. Their colleagues would get fingerprints and see whatever else they could do. They had little hope, however, of finding anything more.

"You'll have to get the money on Monday morning, Madeline,"

Woolcott was saying, as Hudson walked into the room. “We’ll just keep it here until they tell us where to deliver it.”
Jones left the office.

Übung 40: Setzen Sie die Wörter in Klammern in die entsprechenden Lücken ein!
(president, brilliant, businessman, adequate, member, collects)

“I’ll send someone with her when she 1. collects the money.” Hudson said. “Now, what can you tell me about Greenwood?” he asked.

“Career engineer, started here at 24 and worked his way up to 2. president. Not a 3. brilliant engineer, but a very good 4. businessman.”

“And Marvin Good?”

“I lured him away from Spirit Mark, the sports car manufacturer, one of our competitors. It wasn’t too difficult, since we have more interesting work for him here.”

“And Donleavy?”

“Donleavy’s a good engineer, an 5. adequate businessman, a satisfactory director of R&D. He’s also a 6. member of a motorcycle gang.”

"Donleavy's in a gang?" Hudson asked, surprised.
"Well, they are not Hell's Angels, as you can judge by looking at Donleavy, but he's a member of a group known as the Shufton Elite."
"I've heard of them. They've had difficulties with the police in the past. He's a member of the Shufton Elite? I'd have never for a moment connected Donleavy with a motorcycle gang. Bowling or chess I would have expected, but not motorcycles."
"I'm not trying to suggest that Donleavy has had any run-ins with the police, Inspector. There are plenty of peaceful members of motorcycle gangs, I suppose."
"It's a way of life," Hudson agreed, "an alternative lifestyle, as we say today. Even so –. I need your home phone number, Mr Woolcott, because we may have to prepare for Monday."

Woolcott picked a business card up from a box on his desk, wrote on it quickly and handed it to Hudson. On the way out of Woolcott's office, Hudson asked Jagger for Donleavy's home address.

"You're calling me on a Friday night?" Elvira Elliot asked. "I thought you would be out with some beautiful criminal trying to learn all her secrets."
"There's only me and Miss Paddington, Elvira, and she's already in her bed reading."
"Well, I'm meeting some friends in a pub in a little while. You're welcome to join us."
"No, thanks. I'm calling on business, to ask you a question about insurance."
"That's my speciality, Jimmy. What would you like to know?"
"You're feeling quite cheery tonight."
"Why not? Now, if you're not going to join us, ask me your question so I can get ready to go out. I've got to make myself presentable."

"That won't take very long, Elvira."
"Such a sweetheart, Jimmy, you could almost break a girl's heart."

Übung 41: Welcher Satz enthält die richtige Übersetzung? Kreuzen Sie an!

1. I'm trying to learn all your secrets.
   a) ☐ Ich versuche, hinter alle Ihre Geheimnisse zu kommen.
   b) ☐ Ich versuche, von Ihren Geheimnissen zu lernen.
   c) ☐ Ich versuche, etwas über Ihre Geheimnisse zu lernen.

2. Where did you learn that habit?
   a) ☐ Wo hast Du diese Gewohnheit erlernt?
   b) ☐ Wo hast Du von dieser Gewohnheit erfahren?
   c) ☐ Wo hast Du Dir das angewöhnt?

3. We learnt how to write business letters.
   a) ☐ Wir haben erfahren, wie man Geschäftsbriefe schreibt.
   b) ☐ Wir haben gelernt, wie man Geschäftsbriefe schreibt.
   c) ☐ Wir haben verstanden, wie man Geschäftsbriefe schreibt.

4. Hudson learned that she was an insurance specialist.
   a) ☐ Hudson erfuhr, dass sie eine Versicherungsexpertin ist.
   b) ☐ Hudson hat bei ihr Versicherungsfachmann gelernt.
   c) ☐ Hudson hat gelernt, dass sie Versicherungsexpertin ist.

"What happened to 'James'?"
"We retired him. He's not good company on a Friday night, too stiff."
"Right. Correct me if I'm wrong, Elvira, but there's insurance against kidnapping, isn't there?"

"That's not one of the big sellers, but it does exist."
"Is it expensive?"
"Premiums vary, naturally."
"How would I find out if A&L have kidnapping insurance and where or when they opened the policy?"
"Ask them."
"If I wanted to avoid that route?"
"Call around. Perhaps you'll get lucky and one of the hundreds of insurance companies will recognise A&L as one of their customers. Or see if they file a claim after paying a ransom."
"You've been very helpful, Elvira."
"It's only purchased by companies operating in dangerous regions – in the Middle East, for instance. Are you sure you won't join us? It'd be nice to see you again. I haven't seen you in ages, and you won't be 35 forever."
"I haven't been 35 in a long time. Enjoy yourself this evening, Elvira."
"Will do."

ÜBUNG 42 !

Übung 42: Was wird hier beschrieben? Setzen Sie die Wörter in Klammern richtig ein!
(premium, insurance specialist, insurance company, insurance policy, over-insured, insurance agent)

1. A contract of insurance is called an ____________.

2. If you have too many insurances you are ____________.

3. A company engaged in the business of insuring is an ____________.

4. A person employed to collect premiums door to door is an

insurance agent.

5. An amount to be paid for a contract of insurance is a

premium.

6. A person trained in the branch of insuring is an

insurance specialist.

"Don't sulk so," Miss Paddington said to Hudson as she brought him a plate with two boiled eggs and beans on toast. "It's Saturday morning."
"I'm just feeling thoughtful, Miss Paddington. I'm not sulking."
"If you say so. What's the problem?"
"This kidnapping case I'm working on."
"From what I know, there's always a reason why kidnappers take someone hostage – usually it's for money but not always."
"Is that what you read in your crime novels?"
"It's what I see on television too, James. The news may be all bad, but nevertheless you can learn a lot about the reasons why people do things."
"They want £200,000."
"That's not very much by today's standards," Miss Paddington observed. "If that's all they asked for, they probably want something else. I read a novel recently where a character was kidnapped because he knew government secrets. They tortured him while negotiating with the government for money. They really planned on killing him once they got the information they needed, and then using this information to bring the government down. It was a power-hungry member of the opposition party."

Übung 43: Wie lauten die Sätze in der richtigen Reihenfolge?

1. negotiating were ransom they the

Were they negotiating the ransom

2. was complicated a case Hudson on working kidnapping

Hudson was working on a complicated kidnapping

3. business the thing only was on mind his

The only thing on mind was business

4. not why the hostage only is kidnappers reason money someone take

5. were killing hostage the planning kidnappers on the

"Miss Paddington, can we talk about something besides these horrid books you read?"

"You needn't get in a huff. You know as well as anyone how accurate they are."

"They're only fantasy, Miss Paddington. If any of your crime novelists had ever worked a day as a bobby or in a constabulary's office, they might learn the way we really work."

"I try to help and you get all in a huff."

"First I'm sulking, now I'm in a huff. Miss Paddington, you are impossible this morning. But," he added, after taking a sip of coffee, "breakfast is good."

Inspector Hudson got in his Bentley. He pulled out his mobile phone and dialled Malcolm Evans's number.
"Evans."
"Evans, this is Inspector Hudson. You have any plans for the day?"
"I'm spending it with my girlfriend."
"You're spending it with me."
"Anything to do with Donny?"
"Naturally."
"Okay."

Übung 44: Setzen Sie die Adverbien in die entsprechenden Lücken ein!
(firstly, secondly, away, quickly, down, back, somewhere)

The door to the Bentley opened and a young woman looked in.

"See, a real, live Scotland Yard Inspector. Just like I said." The woman backed 1. __away__ and let Evans get in. He rolled the window 2. __down__ and said, "I'll give you a ring when I get 3. __back__."

Hudson drove away 4. __quickly__.

"Is that your girlfriend?"

"Yes. She thought I had another date. She couldn't believe that I would be going 5. __somewhere__ with a Scotland Yard Inspector."

"She's very pretty, Evans. You've got good taste."

Evans frowned at Hudson. "So, where are we going?" he asked.

"To St Albans."

"To VF? You think they have Donny?"

"I don't know what's going on yet. I'm just looking into a possibility."

"Do you think he's in St Albans?"

"Donny, I believe, he is somewhere in Soho."

"Then why are we going to St Albans."

"6. Firstly ____, we can't do a building to building search of Soho for Mr Award. 7. Secondly ____, I've never been there, Evans. And, whoever has Donny took him for a reason. Perhaps it has something to do with the new engine; perhaps not."

"This new engine could put A&L into the lead."
"Indeed. And if A&L became the market leader, then what would happen to VF?"
"They would have to come up with something new, which means they would have to put more money into research and rush something onto the market."

Evans was giving Hudson directions to the VF headquarters in St Albans. "I know we go west on King Harry Lane. After that we should see it. There's the Abbey Church of St Alban."
The two men looked at the cathedral towering over the city.
"So, I heard that Donleavy's a member of the Shufton Elite."
"He may not look it, Inspector, but he's a tough man. He may be short and funny looking, but he's strong. Once he and Donny

almost came to blows and he picked up part of an engine that Donny and I had had to carry together. He threw it at Donny."

"He's a little violent, then?"

"Oh, he apologized later – because he broke the part. Donny's what I call a 'divider'. Because of the way he is, you either like him or you hate him. Donleavy hates him, but he knows Donny's a talented engineer. You don't have to like everyone you supervise, do you? You don't think that Donleavy kidnapped Donny, do you, Inspector?"

"Perhaps members of the Shufton Elite are doing Donleavy a favour or taking revenge for him. Stranger things have happened."

Übung 45: Bilden Sie die erste Steigerungsform der Adjektive!

ÜBUNG 45 !

1. successful more successful
2. many much
3. funny funnier
4. violent ______
5. late later
6. talented ______

"You're dreaming, Inspector. Donleavy's a rather simple fellow. His world is black and white, good and bad, right and wrong. His is the simplest world picture I've ever come upon."

"Right. Donny Award – bad. Then everything is justified for Donleavy."

They found the VF headquarters. As it was Saturday, it looked deserted.

"Shall we go inside?"
"Are you crazy, Inspector? I'm not going in there. I work for A&L. What would I be doing in there?"
"Quite right." Hudson drove a short distance away and parked the car off the street, attempting to hide it. "Here's my card. Call Scotland Yard if I don't come back."
"Do you mind if I ask what you're doing here?"
"Yes, I do."

When Hudson returned, he was a bit out of breath and his suit was dirty. He started the Bentley hastily and pulled away quickly.
"What was that all about?" Evans asked.
"Just protecting you."
"Protecting me?"

ÜBUNG 46 !

Übung 46: Beantworten Sie die Fragen zum Text!

1. Where did Hudson and Evans go?

They go to the VT headquater

2. Why did they go there?

3. What did Evans tell Inspector Hudson about Donleavy?

4. Did Hudson think Donleavy was suspicious?

5. Why didn't Evans want to go into the VF headquarters with the Inspector?

Because he works for A&L.

"Yes, there were security guards following me. They didn't approve of my presence on company grounds. I looked around a bit, managed to get inside, but I didn't see any sign of Mr Award."

"You didn't really expect to."

"No, I didn't."

"Then what was the point?"

"I'm just heating things up, Mr Evans."

"Heating things up?"

"Have you ever noticed how some people can deal well with stress and others, especially beginners, can't deal with it? And when they're under stress, they make mistakes. There it is again, the Abbey at St Alban."

They were back in London, amidst the weekend traffic.

"Can you tell me about Madeline Jones?"

"She's a snake in the grass."

"I am familiar with the expression, but tell me what you mean."

"She just seems to do Woolcott's dirty work. She just seems to be everywhere, watching everyone."

"She's his eyes and ears."

"And teeth. Sometimes Donleavy comes back with something you said, and we all know that it came to him via Madeline Jones."

"How often have you seen Woolcott?"

"I've never met him. Donny met him recently, but that was because of the new engine."

"I thought you were part of that."

"I don't care about recognition. I learn a lot working with Donny. That makes my work interesting, the rest is just gravy."
"Yes, but we could all do with a little gravy, especially if it comes in the form of pound coins."

ÜBUNG 47

Übung 47: Welche Übersetzung der Redewendungen stimmt? Kreuzen Sie an!

1. She's a snake in the grass.
   a) ☐ Sie kommt überall durch.
   b) ☒ Sie ist gefährlich.
   c) ☐ Sie ist eine falsche Schlange.

2. She's his eyes and ears.
   a) ☐ Er hat Augen und Ohren nur für sie.
   b) ☐ Sie ist seine bessere Hälfte.
   c) ☒ Sie ist seine Spionin.

3. Fortune favours fools.
   a) ☒ mehr Glück als Verstand haben
   b) ☐ Einer ist immer der Dumme.
   c) ☐ Dumm gelaufen!

On Sunday, Hudson gave Woolcott a ring at his home.
"We are going to have to do some negotiating tomorrow, Mr Woolcott," Hudson said, "with the kidnappers."
"I think it's better if you do the talking this time."
"You're an experienced negotiator, Mr Woolcott. This should be your area of expertise."
"I negotiate with money, not peoples' lives."

"It's always peoples' lives, Mr Woolcott. But I understand that you see it differently."
"What do you have planned?"
"We're going to smoke them out."
"What do you mean?"
"Just what I said. You'll see tomorrow. Until then, Mr Woolcott."

While Hudson's associates from Scotland Yard were setting up their equipment in Woolcott's office on Monday morning, Hudson went down to visit Donleavy. He passed Madeline Jones, who flashed a very small, quick smile at him, but didn't slow down.
Hudson stopped and turned around. "Pardon, Ms Jones? I say, Ms Jones." Jones continued walking. Hudson ran after her, stopping her with a hand on her forearm. "Ms Jones, when I call you, I expect you to stop and listen to me. You and I are going to the bank together at 10.30 am. I'll meet you in your office in exactly twenty minutes. Be ready."
"I have a meeting," she said, smiling supremely.
"It's postponed – even if it is with Mr Woolcott. Get everything you need to withdraw the money, including a briefcase to carry the money. I'll be in your office in twenty minutes," he repeated and then walked back towards the R&D Department.

Übung 48: Ordnen Sie die Buchstaben zu sinnvollen Wörtern!

ÜBUNG 48!

1. ratenotogi (Unterhändler) negotiator
2. esitrxepe (Fachgebiet) expertise
3. metnartped (Abteilung) department
4. stoppone (verschieben) postpone

5. remeluspy (überlegen) ________________

6. sacreibfe (Aktentasche) ________________

"Did you just receive a visit from Madeline Jones?" Hudson asked Donleavy, as he walked into the latter's office.
"Yes. I am always receiving visits from Ms Jones. All directors do. Vice presidents too, if they are unfortunate."
"Did she have some information for you?"
"She is Woolcott's bearer of bad news. Our sales are down for this quarter. Share prices are fluctuating, which generally means they are slipping."
"And what does that have to do with R&D?"
"We've got a new clutch connection that will get our cars up to higher speeds faster. He wants it in production so we can put it on this year's models and offer it to those driving our cars. We planned on releasing it onto the market next summer. Woolcott says that this clutch will bring a quicker return on our investment than Award's engine will. I think Award's engine ensures our long-term viability as a company. He sees it only as a vulnerability. Standing still makes you more vulnerable than anything else."

ÜBUNG 49 !

Übung 49: Übersetzen Sie!

1. Aktienpreise share prices
2. schwankend fluctuating
3. Kabel ________________
4. auf den Markt bringen onto the market
5. Investition investment viability

6. Existenzfähigkeit vulnerability

"I hear you're a member of the Shufton Elite."
Donleavy, a short man with a small round face and a long nose and chin, stood as tall as he could.
"And what exactly do you mean by that?"
"Nothing."
"Now, Inspector Hudson, aren't you supposed to be trying to find the kidnappers? What are you doing spending your time around here asking questions? Am I a suspect in the kidnapping of one of my own employees?"
"An employee that you didn't like."
"I don't take kindly to threats, sir!"
"That wasn't a threat, Mr Donleavy, that was a fact. I don't threaten lightly, sir!"
As Hudson left the room, he heard Donleavy say, "If it's not Woolcott or Jones or Greenwood, now it's Inspector Dimwit from Scotland Yard."

Übung 50: Setzen Sie die richtige Präposition in die entsprechende Lücke ein!
(up, at, from, over, at, in, to, with)

Hudson drove a very quiet Madeline Jones to the Bank of Greater London. She had 1. with ________ her a briefcase and Woolcott's card which would allow her access to the bank accounts. Close 2. to ________ busy Oxford Street, Hudson parked the car, and they got out and walked to the bank.

"Should anyone attempt to take the briefcase 3. ________ you once we have the money," Hudson said, "I suggest you immediately throw yourself to the ground. I'm carrying a weapon, and I will be shooting 4. ________ whoever makes the attempt. I would prefer not to shoot 5. ________ you."

"Is that supposed to make me feel more secure? Besides, I thought you didn't carry weapons."

They entered the bank and walked 6. ________ to a small desk. Jones picked up a withdrawal form and began to fill it 7. ________. Hudson followed her up to a cashier where she handed the form 8. ________.

The cashier looked at the form and then asked, "How do you want it?"

"In small notes," said Jones, "but not too small. I have to carry it."

"Are twenty pound notes all right?"

Jones looked at Hudson, who nodded his head. "Yes, that'll do."

They left the bank and walked down Oxford Street quickly. The pavement was crowded with summer shoppers and tourists.

Hudson kept very close to Jones, occasionally pressing against her shoulder.

"Must you be so close to me?"

"Trust me, if these kidnappers are really dangerous, you don't want me any farther away from you than I am at this moment."

"If it's that dangerous, it would have been better not to bring me at all."

"Someone had to withdraw the money, Ms Jones."
"So there's at least one thing that a Scotland Yard Inspector can't do."
"Congratulations, you've found my weakness at last."

Übung 51: Welche Wörter gehören zusammen? Kreuzen Sie das jeweils richtige Wort an!

1. bank
   a) ☒ cashier
   b) ☐ carrier
   c) ☐ shopper

2. kidnapping
   a) ☒ ransom
   b) ☐ clutch
   c) ☐ tourists

3. Scotland Yard
   a) ☒ weakness
   b) ☐ congratulations
   c) ☒ suspect

They made it back to the A&L offices without incident and then, along with Woolcott, Jagger, Donleavy, Greenwood and Hudson's associates, they began to wait for the call.
"I don't expect they'll be on time this time either," one of Hudson's associates, a junior inspector, said.
A church bell outside marked off each quarter hour and then rang one o'clock.

"Well, it's one o'clock," said Woolcott, "it doesn't appear they're going to call." He stood and pulled on his jacket. "I've got other work to do, so if you don't mind –"

"We're talking about a man's life, here, Mr Woolcott," said Hudson. "We have got to sit here all afternoon, if that's what it takes, until they call. If you're not here, we can't do anything."

"I'm not going to sit here and do nothing."

"Good idea. Do something at your desk. Ms Jagger, I would like to see the company file on Donald Award please."

"That's not …," began Woolcott, and then broke off when Hudson gave him a questioning look.

ÜBUNG 52

Übung 52: Kreuzen Sie die richtige Bedeutung der Sätze an!

1. If you don't mind, I'm going to get back to work.
   - a) ☐ If you take a nap, I'll go to work again.
   - b) ☐ If you can't think, then I'll do the work.
   - c) ☒ If you have nothing against it, I'll start working again.

2. Where is my mind today?
   - a) ☒ I can't concentrate today.
   - b) ☐ Please help me; I lost my mind this morning.
   - c) ☐ You're distracting me.

3. Do you mind if I smoke?
   - a) ☐ Will you watch me smoke?
   - b) ☒ Will it bother you if I smoke?
   - c) ☐ Will you be able to think if I smoke?

4. I'm of two minds on this issue.

a) ☒ I have two opinions on this subject.

b) ☐ I agree with you and with myself.

c) ☑ I can't make up my mind about this subject.

He nodded to Jagger, who went out into the other office and pulled a file out of one of the large filing cabinets. "Here it is," she said. Hudson started to read through the file. "£45,000 a year salary," he said aloud, "not bad at all. But maybe not good enough for such a talented engineer. Look at that, he had just been given a pay rise to £45,000 a year when he was kidnapped. A £5,000 a year salary increase isn't bad. I reckon he hasn't yet got the money from his pay rise. What does the average worker in the plant make?"

"Wages depend upon experience and the role within the plant or on the assembly line."

"Just a general figure," said Hudson.

"Somewhere around £20,000 a year. It doesn't sound like much, but you did ask for an average."

"It looks like Mr Award was a productive engineer but produced a few too many hate mails," Hudson said, holding up a sheet of paper with an email on it. "Do you routinely go through employee emails?"

"No, we don't," Woolcott answered angrily. "We probably received a complaint about a letter he wrote. That's the only reason I can think of for going through his or any employee's files."

"I can see why you saved this one. It's a gem."

Hudson read:

Dear Michael,

Thank you for sending the wrong part once again. In the future I'll order the part right next to the one I want and perhaps then I'll get what I need. I am returning the part today and expect to have the postage subtracted from our account. Please send No. 13334A (rather than No. 13335A which has a different diameter) ASAP.

Regards

Donald Award

"I do hope that he is being a bit more diplomatic at the moment," Hudson said in conclusion.
"There shouldn't be any objections to Donleavy, Greenwood, and Jagger going about their business, Inspector?"
"None at all."

ÜBUNG 53 !

Übung 53: Ordnen Sie die Buchstaben zu einem sinnvollen Wort!

1. Money paid to factory workers is called (esagw) wages.
2. To send a product back is to (trrneu) return it.
3. Another word for a factory is (tlpna) plant.
4. Money paid to office workers is called (ylraas) salary.
5. An argument against an action or decision is an (noojbteci) objection.
6. A customer may (ncmiaplo) __________ if a service does not meet expectations.

The three left the office, so only Woolcott, Jones, the two assistants from Scotland Yard and Hudson were left in the room.

Hudson sat silently in his seat until half past five when he left the office for a moment. The others had been in and out for visits to the lavatory, but had remained at their posts most of the time. Hudson had suddenly remembered the numbers he had found on Jones' telephone.

He dialled the first number.

"Hello," a male voice said. It sounded as if he had rung up a private residence.

"I'm sorry; I must have dialled the wrong number. Is this –," Hudson read the number, "or did I indeed dial wrong?"

"That's the number."

"I was calling for a Donald Award."

"Never heard of him." There was a pause.

"Could you tell me who I have reached?" Hudson asked.

"You haven't reached the person you were trying to call," the voice said and hung up the phone.

Übung 54: Welche Wörter gehören in die Lücken?
(confirmation, reservations, return, dialled, following)

ÜBUNG 54 !

He (1.) __________ the second number, one that had appeared twice.

"Executive Travel," a woman's voice said.

"I'm calling about Mr Woolcott's (2.) __________," Hudson said.

"We have no reservations for a Mr Woolcott," the voice said after a moment.

"I'm sorry. They must be under Jones, Madeline Jones."

"Okay," she said after a moment. "We have two tickets to Bermuda."

"(3.) ______?"

"Yes. You fly out Friday and return the (4.) ______ Sunday. Do you want your (5.) ______ number?"

"No thanks, my wife must have it."

"Thank you for calling."

"Thank you."

Suddenly, at the other end of the corridor, Jones left Woolcott's office, so Hudson was forced to stop.

"This is rather silly, Mr Hudson. I must protest against this waste of time."

"Do you know for certain that the kidnappers are not going to call?"

"Don't you think they would have called by now if they were going to?"

"We're at their mercy."

"We're at your mercy," she answered.

Hudson walked into Woolcott's office.

"What do you think, Johnson?" he asked his junior associate.

"They'll probably call tomorrow, but you never can tell. They could try and call tonight at eleven."

Hudson looked at Woolcott, who also looked ill-tempered.

"What do you think, Mr Woolcott? Should we call it a day?"

"I suggested that several hours ago," he said, standing up.

"I'll take that for a yes."

"You've wasted a good part of my day."

"In a good cause, Mr Woolcott."
"That's debatable, Inspector."
"I would call Award's life a good cause, wouldn't you, Mr Woolcott?"
"Of course," he said, sounding a little humbled.

Übung 55: Beantworten Sie die Fragen zum Text!

1. Is Mr Award an ideal employee?

___

2. Why does Inspector Hudson read Award's employee file?

___

3. Is Mr Award's letter diplomatic?

___

4. Whose telephone does Inspector Hudson take phone numbers from?

___

5. Are employee files usually supposed to remain confidential?

___

"You should have seen it, Miss Paddington," Hudson said, as she brought the evening meal to the table. "It was almost as if he knew they weren't going to call."
"Not a very good boss, having your own employees kidnapped."
"I'm not sure that's what has happened," he said, stabbing food with

his fork, "but something strange was going on and I played right along. It was like free jazz or an impromptu performance on stage."
"What did you do then, James?"
"I made Woolcott stay in his office. I sat with him all afternoon. I felt like a headmaster with a naughty pupil."
"That might have been fun for you, James, but think of the poor lad held hostage."
"Miss Paddington, there was nothing else I could do for him. The kidnappers never called. We waited more than five hours."
"I don't blame you, James. I don't hold you responsible. It's sad."
"The worst thing about kidnappings is that you can only wait. You wait until you get told what to do. Then you can finally make a move. Until then, it's just sit and sit some more – and try to be patient."
"Which is just what the poor boy is doing, only he doesn't have it so comfortable."

ÜBUNG 56 !

Übung 56: Welches Wort ist das „schwarze Schaf"?

1. wages, pay, salary, profit
2. letter, bill, email, message
3. confidential, secret, private, confident
4. polite, direct, diplomatic, tactful
5. dial, ring, hang up, call,
6. impromptu, organised, planned, intentional

The following morning, Hudson quickly dropped by his office on the way to A&L. He had a message to call Sir Reginald.
"Hello."
"Hello, Sir Reginald, Hudson here."

"Hello, James. I've already had a call this morning from Martin Woolcott. He's rather annoyed that he had to spend the entire afternoon yesterday waiting for a telephone call that never came."
"They said they'd call Monday at noon and didn't."
"He says he feels he's being treated like a suspect, James."
"Everybody is a suspect. You know how complicated these cases can be. You said so yourself."
"I didn't say it was an inside job," Sir Reginald said, "I only said I thought it would be complicated."
"And it is."
"Just do me a favour, James, please."
"Yes, sir. Anything."
"Take a little heat off of Woolcott."
"I'll see what I can do."
"Thank you, James."
"Don't mention it, Sir Reginald."

Übung 57: Setzen Sie die Sätze in die indirekte Rede!

1. "I think it will be complicated," I said.

   I said I thought it would be complicated.

2. "I think it is a waste of time," she said.

   She said I thought it was a waste of time

3. "We want more money," the kidnappers said.

   The k said

4. "Award always goes to a pub after work," Evans said.

   E said Award always went to a pub after work

5. “We’ll call on Monday,” they said.

Hudson quickly left the office and drove to A&L’s offices. Everything in Woolcott’s office was set up for the call. The difficulty is, Hudson thought, that if it is someone from within A&L who organised this whole thing, then he or she knows our every move, always knows our next move. Somehow I have to keep them guessing. It is time for Inspector Hudson from Scotland Yard to play a bit more of an aggressive role than I’ve played so far – although this case has already forced me to behave differently. Negotiators must have all the tools of the trade at hand.

Übung 58: Bringen Sie die Sätze des Telefonats in die richtige Reihenfolge!

1. “Would you like to leave a message?”
2. “Yes, this is Inspector Hudson.”
3. “A&L Automobiles, may I help you?”
4. “Please tell him to call me as soon as possible.”
5. “He’s not in the office at the moment.”
6. “I would like to speak with Mr Woolcott, please.”

Lösung: ______

The call came almost on time, just a few minutes after noon.
“Good afternoon,” said the caller, a bit more confident than the first day. “We have decided to increase the ransom. To double it. We want £400,000 now.”
Hudson looked at Woolcott, whose face was unreadable.

"We waited for you all day yesterday," Woolcott said, finally.
"I don't care about that."
"And where do you want the £400,000 delivered?" Hudson asked.
"Who is that? That's not Mr Woolcott's voice."
"It doesn't matter. When and where do you want the money delivered?"
"Just get the money, and we'll call you tomorrow with the details."
"How do we know that Donald Award is still alive?"
"Trust me, he's still alive."
"But I don't trust you," Hudson said.
"Don't worry," the caller said, irony in his voice, "he feels at home where he is."
"I want to hear his voice," Hudson insisted. "If you can't prove he's alive, there's no point in this continuing. We won't deliver the money until we know for certain that he's still alive."
"You don't make the rules."
"You have Donald Award. We have the £400,000. You have something we want, and we have something you want. Now, if you want the money, we need proof that Award is still alive – it's that simple. We're not giving you all this money for a dead engineer."
A stone-cold silence filled the room for a moment. The telephone was as if dead too.
"Do we have a deal?" Hudson asked, finally breaking the silence.
"Okay, okay," said the caller, sounding annoyed. "We'll have proof that Award is still alive when we call you tomorrow."
"Good." Hudson said, "And try to be a bit more punctual tomorrow. We would like to conclude this business as quickly as possible."
"We'll call tomorrow morning at 10 am," the caller said, even more annoyed. "You be ready for us." The phone line went dead.
"I guess that's it for today," Hudson said.
"You were hard on him, sir," the assistant named Johnson said.

"Don't feel sorry for him, he's holding hostage a young man only a couple of years older than you."

"I hope you weren't too hard," said Woolcott. "I hope they aren't hard on Award because of your demands."

"I doubt they will be. Besides, they doubled the ransom, so they made a demand of their own. My request for proof that Award is still alive was only a counter-demand."

ÜBUNG 59 !

Übung 59: Welche Synonyme gehören zusammen? Setzen Sie die richtige Ziffer ein!

1. demand	☐ prompt
2. conclude	☐ evidence
3. annoyed	☐ insist
4. deal	☐ subordinate
5. punctual	5 terminate
6. assistant	☐ irritated
7. proof	4 agreement

Woolcott left his office and Hudson remained behind while the two assistants gathered up their equipment.

"Why do you think they doubled the ransom?"

"They're getting better at this hostage game probably," Hudson answered.

"Not a whole lot better," remarked the other. "£400,000 is still not a lot of money for a ransom. We've seen much higher."

"So, will I see you two here tomorrow morning bright and early?"

"No, sir. We have a different assignment tomorrow. You'll probably have Elaine Dinsmore."

"One woman for the two of you. That shows just how much the

Yard thinks of you. She has been trained for this, then, I suppose?"
"Yes. She's good. She beat Johnson kick-boxing last Thursday."
"That was supposed to remain between us," Johnson said.
"She's a colleague. Besides, …"
"That's enough. Where was the caller calling from?" Hudson asked.
"Somewhere in Uxbridge. A couple of agents are driving there to see what they can find, but you know they're not going to get much."
"I don't think they're keeping him in London," Hudson said.

Übung 60: Unterstreichen Sie die richtige Alternative!

ÜBUNG 60 !

Back at Scotland Yard, Hudson found a (1.) paper/message from Elvira. He dialled her (2.) extension/indirect number.
"Elvira Elliot."
"Ms Elliot, (3.) that/this is Inspector Hudson, Scotland Yard."
"James. You're returning my call. So nice of you."
"The least I could do."
"I (4.) answered/called you because I took a personal and professional risk for you this morning."
"What do you mean?"
"I (5.) dialled/called A&L and attempted to sell them ransom insurance."
"Who did you (6.) speak/talk with?"
"I spoke with a John Greenwood, president in charge of manufacturing and quality control. His department also handles insurance for the entire company. As you can imagine, he was a bit suspicious. But I mentioned the kidnapping this past spring of Rosemary Kay. Remember? Gabriel Aurochs, the Greek tycoon, kid-

napped her when she successfully prevented his hostile takeover bid for her company. He remembered it, and then said they had no kidnapping insurance and didn't want or need any."

"Thank you, Elvira. That was very kind of you, not to mention risky."

"For a friend like you, James, I'd do just about anything."

" We're back on 'James' again, are we?"

" 'Jimmy' just doesn't (7.) pass/suit you, even on a warm Friday evening with a full moon shining."

"Right. Well, thanks (8.) again/more for your help, Elvira."

"My pleasure."

Hudson walked into Sir Reginald's office, interrupting him at work.

"I could do with a break," Sir Reginald said. He ordered a pot of tea and then asked Hudson, "So, what can I do for you?"

"I'm slowly making progress on this kidnapping case."

"Good to hear."

"Johnson and his associate said they've been assigned to another case as of tomorrow, is that right?"

"It is. I've assigned Elaine Dinsmore to you. She's a junior inspector, just like they are."

"Why just one young woman, when before I had two young men?"

"Because Ms Dinsmore is quite enough. Those two comedians, Johnson and Harrison, should be posted to a danger-free zone. If we had an office in the arctic regions, I believe I'd send them there."

"Well, then I'm glad to have Ms Dinsmore. Could you make sure she's notified that I'll pick her up here tomorrow at 7.30 am?"

"Of course. So," Sir Reginald asked, "what's your next step?"

"Tomorrow morning we get more money and then we pay the ransom."

"Just try to avoid a shoot-out. We lose more agents and hostages that way."
"Will do."
"Help yourself to sugar, James."

Übung 61: Setzen Sie die fehlenden Präpositionen ein!

1. He was assigned ______ a new project.
2. I'm making progress ______ this report.
3. He's working ______ A&L.
4. We have offices ______ Europe and Asia.
5. I would like to speak ______ Mr Woolcott.
6. She thinking ______ transferring to another department.
7. Please call back ______ the morning.

The following morning, at 7.30 am sharp, Hudson drove his Bentley in front of the Scotland Yard offices. It was a clear, sunny day. Out of the entrance ran a young woman with shoulder-length curly blond hair, carrying a briefcase. She looked powerful, though her voice when he heard it was rather soft.
"Good morning, Inspector Hudson," she said, getting into his car. "I'm Elaine Dinsmore."
"Good morning, Dinsmore. We have a lot to cover this morning. I suppose you received an update on the case."
"Yes, I did."
"Then the first course of action is to collect the additional £200,000 and then to negotiate with hostage-takers. I want to know

the location of the caller or callers. Does that sound like a good morning's work?"

The young woman nodded to say yes in answer to his question and then looked silently out the window.

ÜBUNG 62

Übung 62: Wie lauten die Sätze in der richtigen Reihenfolge?

1. call later will back just I

I will just call back later

2. message leave a I may?

May I leave a message?

3. to please Mr Woolcott like speak I'd with

I'd like to speak with Mr. W please

4. Development Malcolm Evans and is this in Research

This is ME in D&R

5. a is meeting in afraid I'm he

I'm afraid he is in a meeting

6. lot moment work a of I at have the

I have a lot of work at the moment.

Both Woolcott and Jones showed up at 9.00 am. Hudson impatiently drove off with Jones and Dinsmore to get the money from the bank.

"The banks don't open until 9.00 am anyway, Inspector Hudson."

This time Hudson was silent, glancing in the rear-view mirror at Jones, who glanced back at him, coolly.
As they had the day before, Hudson parked off Oxford Street, near the bank and they walked to the building. Dinsmore looked at the two of them and when Jones went up to collect the money, she asked Hudson what was going on.

Übung 63: Setzen Sie die Verben in die richtige Zeitform!

"It (seem) 1. __________ you two hate each other."

"I don't know her enough to hate her, Dinsmore. But I'm sure that we should grow to hate each other if we (get) 2. __________ to know each other. But that doesn't matter to me, at the moment. I'm (focus) 3. __________ on the safe release of Donald Award."

"She does seem rather –"

At that moment, Jones turned around and walked back to them.

"Ready, Inspector."

The three (walk) 4. __________ close together back to the car and drove quickly back to the A&L offices, arriving at almost 9.30 am.

"Go and (set) 5. __________ up your equipment, Dinsmore."

Jones (take) 6. __________ the briefcase with the money to Woolcott's office and then (return) 7. __________ to her own office.

Hudson walked into Woolcott's office and, as he was leaving, overheard the secretary, Ms Jagger, on the telephone.

"No, the company retreat has been postponed for at least two weeks. I know this is short notice. You should have heard the week before last. I don't know how you could have been left off the list."
Hudson stood next to her and waited until she hung up the phone.
"So your company retreat has been cancelled?"
"Yes. The company is divided into thirds and each year one third goes on the company retreat."
"Where do you go? Brighton?"
"Not at all, Inspector Hudson. A&L has a castle in Hertfordshire."
"How far from St. Albans?"
"Not far at all. Why?"
"No reason. It's a lovely area for a holiday."
"It's not all holiday. It's work and holiday. Woolcott likes to have the presidents lead walks through the countryside there. It builds team spirit, he says."
"No doubt," Hudson agreed.

Übung 64: Setzen Sie die passenden Fragewörter ein!

1. What is your main product?
2. Where are your primary customers?
3. Where are your headquarters?
4. Who is your CEO?
5. How is business at the moment?
6. How was your turnover last year?

Shortly before 10 am, President Greenwood and Jones entered

Woolcott's office. Together with Hudson and Dinsmore, they waited anxiously for the phone to ring.
At ten o'clock precisely, the phone rang. One ring, then a second, then a third – Hudson signalled and Woolcott hastily picked up the phone with one last glance at Hudson.
"Hello, Dad," said a male voice.
"Marty, this isn't a good time to call. Let me call you back later."

Übung 65: Ordnen Sie den Sätzen die passende Wendung zu! Tragen Sie die richtige Ziffer ein!

1. to take time off	[5] Sales have exploded.
2. to put off	[4] I hung up the phone.
3. to take off	[3] I'm leaving now.
4. to ring off	[1] I need a holiday.
5. to be off	[2] Let's postpone the meeting.

Everybody breathed in and out and then a minute later, the phone rang again. Once more, following Hudson's directions, Woolcott picked up the phone on the third ring.
"So, here we are again," said a voice. "Do you have the money?"
"Yes," said Woolcott, "we have the money."
"Good."
"Do you have proof that Award's still alive?"
"Indeed we do, Inspector. Come here, Award." In the background the sound of a struggle was clearly audible.
"You better get me out of here quick." Award growled. "You better get me –"
"You need any more proof?" the first man's voice asked.

"That sounded like Award," Greenwood said from his seat, across from Woolcott's desk.
"So where do we deliver the money and get Award?"
"We'll call you today at 2 pm on Woolcott's mobile phone and make the exchange soon after. Be on the road driving around Camden, without any police, and we'll call you."
Woolcott gave the number for his mobile phone.

"Good," said Hudson. "But the exchange will take place tomorrow. Call on Woolcott's mobile at 10 am."
"Today at 2 pm," the caller screamed. "It must take place at 2 pm."
"No, tomorrow at 10 am," Hudson said calmly. "The exchange will be made tomorrow."
"What are you doing?" Woolcott growled.
"Have you lost your mind?" Greenwood asked, quietly but forcefully.
"Tomorrow." Hudson insisted. "You want the £400,000 and we want Award," Hudson reminded them.
"You don't seem to want him very badly," the voice said.
"Tomorrow. At 10 am, so it's after rush hour."
"Okay, tomorrow!" The phone line went dead.

ÜBUNG 66 !

Übung 66: Sind folgende Aussagen richtig? Markieren Sie mit richtig ✔ oder falsch – !

1. The kidnappers are happy with developments.
2. Inspector Hudson is easy to negotiate with.
3. The A&L representatives leave the office happily.
4. Hudson makes demands on the kidnappers.
5. Woolcott and the kidnappers agree about Award.

6. Hudson is driving a hard bargain. ☑
7. Hudson doesn't like Award. ☐

"I'm forced to agree with them," Woolcott shouted. "You don't act like you want Award back. What are you doing?"
"Call Sir Reginald and make your complaint. I know exactly what I'm doing. I'm making sure we get Award safely."
Woolcott, Greenwood and Jones stormed out of his office.
"I suppose we should have been the ones to leave," Hudson said to Dinsmore and then asked her, "Where'd they call from?"
"Harrow," Dinsmore answered.
"Northeast London. Don't bother calling it in."
As they passed by Jagger, Hudson asked the name of the castle in Hertfordshire and its location. "Make sure they put the money in the safe," he reminded Ms Jagger. Then they left A&L.

A short time later, Hudson received a call from Sir Reginald on his mobile phone.
"This *is* most unorthodox, Hudson. This is the second time you've made demands on the kidnappers?"
"That's my strategy, sir. Usually the kidnappers are in control, and this time I'm fighting them for control. Whoever is running this thing thought it would be a simple exchange of ransom money and hostage. Well, it's not going to be that way. It's a hard sell this time. I demanded proof Award was alive and now more time."
"Be very careful. Don't push too hard."
"I'm pushing just as hard as I can, sir."
"I can tell. Just make sure things don't blow up in your face."
"That's always a risk. You know that in negotiations, like in poker, you have to see just how far your counterpart is willing to go."
"I don't need to remind you that you're risking other people's lives

too – Award's first and foremost. Be careful with Dinsmore, too. I've got high hopes for her. No unnecessary risks."
"Don't worry, Sir Reginald, you know I'm committed to getting Award back and that I only take necessary risks."

ÜBUNG 67 !

Übung 67: Übersetzen Sie folgende Verkaufsvokabeln!

1. negotiations	Verhandlungen
2. committed	
3. proof	
4. hard sell	~~hart verkaufen~~
5. to persuade	
6. counterpart	Verhandlungspartner

They drove out to the castle. It took more than an hour to find the area and then almost as long to find the castle itself.
"You're not going to just drive right up to it, are you?"
"Of course not. I'm not sure where I'm going to park the car, but we're going to go up to the castle on foot."
Hudson saw a farm not far from the castle. The castle sat on top of a small hill surrounded on three sides by a thin forest.
"We'll just have to take an indirect route and come in from behind," Hudson said. He parked the cark so that it couldn't be seen from the castle, left to speak to the farmer and then returned to Dinsmore.
"The farmer's a nice chap. He says they've been having a good party up there for several days now."
"A couple of motorcycles just drove away," she said.
"Motorcycles? How many people were on the motorcycles?"

"One on each."
"That means that Donleavy is involved. I'd written him off. I didn't think he seemed the type. Well, I was surprised he was even a member of the Shufton Elite, so that explains it."

Übung 68: Wie lauten die Sätze in der richtigen Reihenfolge?

1. moment just a please!

Just a moment please!

2. wait just to have he will

He will just have to wait

3. sale about make I just was to the

4. she speaking to was him it about

She was speaking to him about it

5. now said you low price too just the was

You said the price was just too low now

They walked on a path through the farmer's fields, then entered the forest and turned back to the castle.
"The director of R&D at A&L – sounds like a new language, a modern language that I don't like – the director of R&D is a member of the Shufton Elite."
"They're not harmless," said Dinsmore, "but they're not *that* dangerous."

Quietly and quickly they walked up to the castle.

"Excuse me for asking, Inspector, but just what are we looking for?"

"I believe Donald Award is being held hostage here."

"You think someone is holding Award hostage in a castle owned by A&L. Is that some kind of joke?"

"It might be a joke. The question is, who is the joke on?"

"I don't get your point."

"It's quite simple really. If he's being held in the castle, then someone at A&L is involved."

"They might have broken in."

"What are the chances of a motorcycle gang breaking into a castle that is owned by the company which employs their hostage?"

"Not very high," she admitted.

"Moreover," Hudson added, "I heard Jagger saying today that the company retreat had been cancelled and it was probably cancelled because of this little event."

"Still, it could all just be coincidence."

"Possibly."

Übung 69: Ersetzen Sie die Wörter durch passende Synonyme!

They 1. (went up) __________ the small hill up to the castle grounds and were able to look in through the small windows. The castle wasn't a 2. (especially) __________ old one. Some 3. (well-off) __________ aristocratic landowner had had it built in the 1880s. It resembled a very large house on an estate, 4. (instead of) __________ a castle like Windsor Castle or any of the many castles scattered across the United Kingdom and Europe. In all, it was a very 5. (contemporary) __________ castle.

They kept moving from window to window, looking inside, until they had 6. (inspected) __________ the entire ground floor, but they found nothing.

"If there's anyone here," said Hudson quietly, "then they must be on the first or second floor."
From far off, they could hear the sound of motorcycles. Hudson and Dinsmore moved as quickly as they could to the side of the castle away from the road that led up to the castle grounds. Soon the sound was louder and the two motorcycles Dinsmore had seen leaving were returning loaded down with food and a lot of beer.

Übung 70: Finden Sie ein sinnvolles Gegenteil zu den Wörtern in Klammern!

! ÜBUNG 70

"That's to be expected of bikers," said Hudson. "They're (1. never) __________ beer drinkers."

"It makes them (2. worse) ______________ fighters for a while. They don't feel (3. nothing) ________________. Afterwards, it makes them (4. valuable) ______________ as fighters."

"How do you know that?"

"I grew up in a (5. safe) ______________ neighbourhood."

The two men, wearing black leather trousers with shirts and blue denim jackets, parked their motorcycles and unloaded them. They put everything in a pile and carried it inside in one trip. Hudson ran towards the door and kept the door from closing with his foot.

"We got it, lads," one of them yelled. "She gave us half the money. Now we can party. Tomorrow we get the rest."

"Four motorcycles and one old Ford," said Hudson. "Probably six maybe eight people inside, including Award."

"What do you think is going on?"

"A party, I imagine," Hudson answered.

"Very funny. I mean, who gave them the money?"

"Who had access to it? Woolcott, Jagger and Jones. It must have been Jones acting on Woolcott's orders. I'm sure Jagger doesn't know what's going on."

"Why, because she's a woman?"

"Jones is a woman too. The difference between a secretary and a personal assistant can be quite big. Jones is what is sometimes called a 'girl Friday' – after Robinson Crusoe's helper. She knows more about Woolcott's activities than Jagger does. She probably knows more about Woolcott's activities than he does, if she's good."

"That wouldn't surprise me. She seemed rather sharp."

"She's more than she appears to be. Wait! I hear something coming from the other side, let's go over and listen."

ÜBUNG 71 !

Übung 71: Sind folgende Aussagen richtig? Markieren Sie mit richtig ✔ oder falsch – !

1. A sales rep promotes a company's products. ☑
2. A personal assistant organises the boss's schedule. ☑
3. A sales rep receives wages for his/her work. ☑

4. Men can be secretaries too.

5. Sales reps don't deal directly with people at other companies.

They moved around the side of the castle, keeping close against it.
"Look at all this money, lads. Money and beer. The only thing we don't have is women."
The bikers were playing music loudly when suddenly the phone rang. Someone turned the music down.
"No. No way. We're not doing the exchange at Trafalgar Square. That's a stupid idea. I know there are a lot of people there, but it's not difficult to surround. They can get the police there in no time. They'll trap us easily, and we're not in this to end up behind bars."
"That's going to make me laugh, to see you lot behind bars."
"Must be Award," Hudson said quietly to Dinsmore.
"No. I'm telling you, Trafalgar Square is out. I'll tell you now exactly how it's going to go: we're dropping him off somewhere tied up."
"No you're not!"
"And we're going to tell your Inspector where to pick him up. I'll decide where before I call tomorrow morning. We're doing what you want, but we're doing it our way. We're the ones taking all the risk."

Übung 72: Setzen Sie die Sätze in die direkte Rede!

1. He said the only thing we didn't have was women.

---

2. She said that it was a stupid idea.

____

3. He said he would buy a car next year.

____

4. She said they weren't going to do that.

____

5. He said to drive to London.

____

6. He said he could deliver the hostage by Thursday.

____

They turned the music up, but Hudson and Dinsmore could still hear inside.

"Can you believe that? She wanted to do the exchange at Trafalgar Square. How stupid do you have to be to come up with that idea?"

"You're not tying me up."

"Yes we are. With pleasure."

"No you're not."

"You're doing what we say, Award, because you're in this as deep as we are now."

"Woolcott's going to pay! And Donleavy too!"

"Tomorrow!" the bikers laughed. "Cheers!"

"I'm going to design an engine ten times better than the one A&L has and put them out of business."

"We've heard that enough the last few days, blonde boy."

"But I mean it."

"I know you do. Now put a sock in it before I put my fist in it."

Übung 73: Welche Bedeutung haben folgende Redewendungen? Kreuzen Sie an!

1. Put a sock in it!
   a) ☐ There's too much noise.
   b) ☑ Stop talking.
   c) ☐ You're hungry.

2. Woolcott's going to pay!
   a) ☑ He'll be sorry for what he's done.
   b) ☐ It's his move.
   c) ☐ It's his round.

3. I don't want to be behind bars.
   a) ☐ I'd prefer not to work at a pub.
   b) ☐ I'd prefer not to go to the zoo.
   c) ☑ I'd prefer not to go to jail.

"Let's get back to London," Hudson said.

As they walked past the motorcycles, Hudson paused a moment to write down the number plates. At that moment, one of the bikers walked outside.

"Hey, who do you think you are?" he asked, his voice altered by alcohol.

Hudson turned around and faced him.

The biker didn't notice Dinsmore, who was standing against the castle. She kicked him in the back. A second kick, to the stomach, knocked him to the ground. Her third kick hit him in the face. He lay, in less than three seconds, unconscious.

Hudson looked at her, amazed. "Thank you, Dinsmore," he said quietly. "I suggest we move quickly."

ÜBUNG 74 !

Übung 74: Unterstreichen Sie die vier inhaltlich nicht passenden Sätze!

They ran all the way back to the Bentley. Hudson started the car and drove off as fast as he could. The golf caddy suggested a six iron. At any moment, Hudson expected to see a fleet of motorcycles driving up. The captain on the ship waved to the passengers.
"You didn't expect anything like this, did you?" Hudson asked.
"No, I was just going to assist with a kidnapping negotiation, I thought. Maybe there would be presents and cocktails, perhaps some hors d'oeuvres. I didn't know it was going to be like this."
"I prefer to be out here doing something rather than sitting in the office filling in paperwork. Here, you feel like you're accomplishing something. In the office, you're just doing busy work, waiting until you're needed again. Did I mention that I'm a stamp collector?"

"How are you feeling after your run?" Dinsmore asked him.
"Quite well, thank you, except for the burning in my lungs."
"You're in good shape for a man of forty."
Hudson laughed. "Forty. That was a good year. You did a first-rate job on the biker."
"I was lucky. He didn't see me and he was so drunk that he could barely react."
"That was top quality work, Dinsmore. You moved like a tornado."

ÜBUNG 75 !

Übung 75: Wie antwortet man kurz und höflich? Kreuzen Sie an!

1. You didn't expect anything like this.
   a) ☐ Yes, I didn't.
   b) ☑ No, I didn't.

2. I finished the report early.
   a) ☐ Good work.
   b) ☐ Good time.

3. Have a good holiday!
   a) ☐ No, thank you.
   b) ☐ I will, thank you.

4. Nice to see you!
   a) ☐ Me too.
   b) ☐ Nice to see you too.

5. Are you Melanie Jones?
   a) ☐ I most certainly am not.
   b) ☐ No, I'm not.

Hudson drove the Bentley as fast as he dared back to London. Once traffic picked up, he was forced to slow down. It was clear by then, however, that the motorcycles were not following. The biker who had seen Hudson probably wouldn't remember anything.

Hudson pulled his notebook out of his pocket and handed it and his mobile phone to Dinsmore.

"Dial those numbers and say that you're Madeline Jones. Make your voice a little deeper. Can you try and speak like her?"

"This is Madeline Jones," she said in a poor imitation of Jones' voice.

"You've got to sound natural."

"Hello, my name is Madeline Jones. I was just calling to see how you are doing."

"That's better," Hudson said.

She dialled the first number. "Hello, this is Madeline Jones. Do I

sound strange? It's been a long day. When will I be home? Around 6.30 or so – whenever you see me. Okay, bye."
"That was the boyfriend or the lover or husband. Okay, next one."
She dialled again. "Hello, Madeline Jones here. The dress is ready to be picked up? Great. I'll pop by tomorrow to pick it up. Thanks."
"Does she ever telephone for work?"
"That wasn't as bad as the first call. I wasn't sure I'd get off the phone alive."
"It's just a phone, Dinsmore. They can't get you. Relax. Here we are driving around London on a motorway. Who can get you here?"

! ÜBUNG 76

Übung 76: Bringen Sie die Sätze des Telefonats in die richtige Reihenfolge!

1. "No, that's everything, thank you."
2. "Hello, Woolcott speaking."
3. "Hello, may I speak with John Woolcott please?"
4. "Thank you. Goodbye."
5. "I'll transfer you to him."
6. "Don't hesitate to call if you need more information."
7. "Is there anything else?"

Lösung: ___ ___ ___ ___ ___ ___ ___

She dialled another number. "John Franklin, Jones here."
Hudson's eyes were suddenly very big.
"I sound different? I'm under a lot of stress at the moment, and I'm coming down with something. Yes, the trip to the Bahamas will do me good. Tomorrow afternoon at 5 pm, no, I didn't forget. I was actually just calling to confirm our meeting. Yes, yes, I'll be there

even if I'm on death's door. Until then." Dinsmore rang off. "He's apparently very anxious to see Ms Jones." she said.
"Did he say why?" Hudson asked.
"No, it just sounded as if he thought I was calling to say I wasn't going to go. Or she couldn't go."
"Where are they meeting?"
"At The Dickens on the Strand."
"At the moment, the difficulty is seeing who, if anyone, is the innocent party."
"Innocence is only a question of degree," Dinsmore said quietly.
"How long have you been at the Yard?" Hudson asked.
"Three years."
"Before you get too down on people, remember they can surprise you with their brutality *and* their willingness to do good. It's dangerous to forget that there are two sides to people."
They made their way into central London, arriving at Scotland Yard at the same time as everybody else was leaving.
"I'll see you tomorrow morning about the same time," Hudson said, and they went their separate ways.

Übung 77: Beantworten Sie die Fragen zum Text!

1. Why is Inspector Hudson not behaving as usual?

____

2. How does Inspector Hudson learn about the castle?

____

____

ÜBUNG 77 !

3. Whose voice does Inspector Hudson hear at the castle?

---

4. Do Hudson and Dinsmore meet any of the bikers?

"So, did Dinsmore perform well?" Sir Reginald asked.
"She's got more kick than an old mule." Hudson answered. Sir Reginald frowned. "It's a joke. The expression means that she's got life, but she's so young that she is naturally filled with life. I mean, however, that she can *kick*. I saw her in action."
"What did you do?"
"Well, we went to a castle today." A questioning look crossed Sir Reginald's face. He didn't like mysteries. "I know where Award's being kept. But it was too complicated to simply free him then and there. Normally, I would have tried but – like you said, it's complicated. He'll be free tomorrow, one way or another."

"You look exhausted," Miss Paddington said. "You need a nice hot bath. I've got a savoury pudding in the oven for you as we speak."
"That's the best news I've heard all day."
"How's your case developing? Have you freed the poor lad?"
"No, we haven't freed him. Tomorrow morning we're making the exchange. We get Award and they get £400,000."
"I hope the poor lad can just get on with his life once he's free."
"The 'poor lad', as you call him, is not so poor. He can defend himself. I heard him threatening his kidnappers today."
"It's as I said, James, sometimes kidnappings bring the worst out in people. It's just as I said –"
"Miss Paddington –"
"Yes?"

"I'm going to have a shower now."
"Yes, dear boy, go and have a nice long shower. By the time you're done, your dinner will be waiting for you on the table."

Übung 78: Welche Gegenteile gehören zusammen? Ordnen Sie zu!

1. defend	☐ sweet
2. threaten	[6] reply
3. savoury	☐ straightforward
4. deny	☐ condemn
5. develop	☐ protect
6. question	[5] acknowledge
7. complicated	☐ reduce

Hudson and Dinsmore were not the first to arrive at the A&L offices that morning. Not only was Ms Jagger there, but Ms Jones was there too. Hudson took the opportunity to walk back to the R&D offices with Dinsmore. Donleavy was in his office, sitting at his desk.
"Good morning, sir," Hudson said, standing in front of the secretary's empty desk, looking in through the door at Donleavy.
"What can I do for you, Inspector?" Donleavy asked.
"We are going to exchange the ransom for Award today."
"I wish you the best of luck. I hope no one gets hurt. The company can afford the £200,000."
"It's been doubled."
"That's unusual," Donleavy said. "Still, A&L can afford it."
"I should think that by the beginning of next week he could be back."
"I hope so. I want him back here to finish his project straightaway."

ÜBUNG 79

Übung 79: Welches Wort ist das „schwarze Schaf“?

1. luck, chance, fancy, fortune
2. opening, opportunity, time, chance
3. executive, CEO, manager, foreman
4. computer, desk, stapler, lamp
5. pen, stapler, paper clip, meeting
6. document, story, file, report
7. inspect, control, monitor, examine

Back up in Woolcott’s office, there was a small panic. “Inspector, £200,000 is missing. I swear to you –” Woolcott stopped speaking as he noticed Hudson signalling him to be quiet.
Hudson closed the door. Only he and Dinsmore and Woolcott were in the office.
“Inspector, half the money is missing. I swear to you that I locked it in the safe yesterday morning. I looked in it before I did so and it was all there, I tell you, it was all there.”
“And after you put it in the safe, what did you do?”
“I drove immediately to Scotland Yard to complain about you.”
“A call wouldn’t do? And after that?”
“I came back here. I had work to do.”

ÜBUNG 80

Übung 80: Bringen Sie die Wörter in die richtige Reihenfolge und bilden Sie sinnvolle Sätze!

1. “safe you checked never the?”

you never checked the safe?

“Why should I?”

2. "access safe else anyone have to the does?"

Does anyone lave acess to the safe?

"Only Ms Jagger and Ms Jones. Ms Jagger, come in here."

3. quickly in Jagger Ms came. "Yes, sir."

(quickly Ms Jagger came in. Yes sir.

4. "safe you the open did yesterday?"

Did you open the safe yesterday?

"No, sir."

5. "office anyone into did my else come?"

Did anyone come into my office?

"I don't know. I had to go to the reception area to sign for packages a couple of times, but I was at my desk most of the morning."

Woolcott walked over to his phone. Hudson quickly followed him and put his hand on top of Woolcott's.

"Ms Jagger, I have to ask you to stay. Dinsmore, close the door."

Dinsmore did as she was told, and Hudson thought quickly.

"You left the office yesterday after I did, to drive to Scotland Yard."

"Yes. Right, Ms Jagger?"

"I didn't know where you were going, but you did leave."

"What are we going to do?" Woolcott asked, almost desperate.

"There's no time for this," Hudson said firmly. "We've got to discuss the ransom exchange."

"What about the money?"

"Let's not discuss the money. The question at the moment is: who is coming along?"

! ÜBUNG 81

Übung 81: Stimmen die nebeneinander stehenden Sätze überein? Markieren Sie mit richtig ✔ oder falsch – !

1. I can't afford to eat out./I don't want to eat out. ☐
2. I can't afford the time off./I have too much work to do. ☐
3. She can't afford to be choosy./She has to take what's offered. ☐
4. We can't afford to ignore this opportunity./We had better pass up this opportunity. ☐
5. He can't afford the time./That watch is too expensive. ☐
6. That affords us plenty of time./That gives us a lot of breathing space. ☐

There was a knock at the door. Hudson nodded to Dinsmore to open the door. Madeline Jones leaned her head in.
"Am I interrupting anything?"
"We were just deciding how we are going to do the exchange."
"I thought you discussed that yesterday. You're going to drive around Camden."
"What I mean, Ms Jones, is who is going to go along to hand the money over and pick up Donald Award? Should we do it alone, Dinsmore and I?"
"I see no need for me to be there," Jones declared.
"And you, Mr Woolcott?"
"He is my employee. Perhaps I should go along."
"I don't think that's a good idea, Mr Woolcott," Jones said. "It might be dangerous."
"She has a point," Hudson agreed, "but it is your decision."
"Can you bring him here afterwards?" Woolcott asked.
"No. We'll have to take him in for questioning."
"Well, let's get the money and go," Hudson said.
Woolcott opened the safe and handed the briefcase to Dinsmore.

"Here's my mobile phone, then. They're going to call on it."
"We'll be off then. Wish us luck."

Hudson was driving around Camden when Woolcott's mobile phone rang. He quickly parked the car and answered the phone.

Übung 82: Unterstreichen Sie die sieben Wörter, die falsch geschrieben sind!

ÜBUNG 82 !

"Hello," Hudson said.
"Hello, Inspector. We are going to make this exchange without any games so there'll be no blodshed. We'd love to put a few wholes in Award, but that's not the kind of man we are. Here's the plan and you'd better follow it. First, we're going to drop Award of. Then we're going to meat you a short distance away. You're going to give us the best of our money. One of us will be near Award and in sight of the exchange. If you do anything foolish, Award's going to be what they call in some parts of the world 'Canibal's Delight'. Am I clear?"

"Crystal clear."
"Good. We're going to do the exchange at Barnard Park, right off Caledonian Road. Do you know where that is?"
"Naturally."
"If you're driving north on Caledonian Road, take a right onto Richmond Avenue. Drive past Barnard Park and take a right onto Barnsbury Road. You'll only have to drive a very little way and you'll see us."
"Should be easy."
"Everything clear, then?"

"Quite clear."

"Good, because I would really hate to put holes in Award."

"Oh shut up," Hudson heard in the background. "Shut up about putting holes in me."

"See you in fifteen minutes. Don't be late." The phone went dead.

Fifteen minutes! Hudson thought. We have to hurry. He turned in the direction of Barnard Park. They sat at several lights. When moving, Hudson tried to manoeuvre through traffic, with little success, so he drove through a couple of red lights. They were almost late when they turned onto Richmond Avenue. Hudson drove down the street as fast as he could, then, after turning the corner onto Barnsbury Lane, slowed down and moved forward very slowly. Suddenly, in the park they saw two motorcycles with riders still sitting on them.

"There they are," Hudson said. He grabbed hold of the suitcase and quickly got out of the car. Dinsmore got out too. "Stay with the car," Hudson said. "This money is lost."

ÜBUNG 83 !

Übung 83: Übersetzen Sie die Wörter in Klammern und vervollständigen Sie den Text!

The bikers (1. fuhren) __________ slowly in Hudson's (2. Richtung) __________ while he (3. ging) __________ over to them. They (4. hielten an) __________ and (5. sahen) __________ at each other. Because of their (6. Helme) __________ and sunglasses, Hudson (7. konnte) __________ not see the bikers' faces.

"You have the money?" Hudson lifted the briefcase. "Open it." Hudson opened the case and tilted it in their direction.
"That looks like the rest of it." The biker took the briefcase and very quickly counted the money. "It's here," he said to his counterpart.
"What about Award? Where is he?"
With a black-gloved hand, one of the bikers pointed towards a small park backing on to Richmond Avenue. There, not far from the street, sat Award, struggling. The bikers revved their engines and drove off towards Award, saluted him and left.

Übung 84: Wie antwortet man kurz und höflich? Kreuzen Sie an!

1. How are you?
   a) ☑ Not bad, thank you.
   b) ☐ Terrible.

2. Thank you for your input.
   a) ☐ It was necessary.
   b) ☑ I hope it was helpful.

3. Is everything clear?
   a) ☑ Naturally.
   b) ☐ Yes, thank you.

4. Is your boss in?
   a) ☑ Right over there.
   b) ☐ Yes, she is.

Hudson and Dinsmore ran towards Award. His face was red. Thick silver tape covered his mouth. His face had several days' growth of

beard. His arms were tied behind his back and his feet tied in front of him. His clothes didn't appear particularly dirty, but he smelled.
"That tape." Hudson shook his head.
"That's going to hurt," Dinsmore agreed.
"There's nothing to do but pull it off him," Hudson said. He leaned over and, getting hold of one edge of the tape, pulled as hard and quickly as he could.
Award let out a very loud scream of pain.
"Owwwww!" There was a clean space on his face where there had been stubble.
"I'll get them back one of these days. I'm going to get the whole world back one of these days. Everyone's going to pay!"

ÜBUNG 85 !

Übung 85: Unterstreichen Sie alle Verben und Wendungen, die Bewegungen beschreiben!

Hudson kneeled in the grass and untied Award's feet while Dinsmore untied the rope binding his hands.
"You're free now, Award. Stand up."
"Who are you?"
"I'm Inspector Hudson from Scotland Yard and that's Junior Inspector Dinsmore."
Award looked them over quickly.
"Well, how do we get out of here? I'm not walking home."
"Come," Hudson said and began to lead the way back to his Bentley.
Award got to his feet and joined them.
At his car, Hudson opened the back door for Award, who got in without saying anything.
"You have nothing with you?" Hudson asked.
"No," Award answered.

As they drove away, Hudson said, "We cannot take you home straightaway. We have to go to Scotland Yard and ask you some questions first. A doctor will also have to examine you to make sure you are okay. I hope you have nothing planned for the next few hours, Award."

"I just want to go home. Can you take me to my flat so I can have a bath and change my clothes?"

"We can get a change of clothes but the bath will have to wait." Hudson and Dinsmore looked at each other. "We wish you could have a bath too," Hudson said.

Übung 86: Welche Wörter gehören in die Lücken? Setzen Sie sie in die richtige Zeitform!

(know, find out, come, go, follow, report, discuss, accompany, try)

Hudson drove to Award's flat.

"How did you 1. ____________ I live here?"

"I 2. ____________ here with Malcolm Evans, to 3. ____________ to 4. ____________ why you were kidnapped and to figure out where."

Hudson and Dinsmore 5. ____________ Award to his flat. They 6. ____________ him inside.

"It smells in here," Award said.

"Just get some clothing. We've got to get going."

Hudson called Sir Reginald to 7. ____________ that Award was now safely in their hands. Next, Hudson called Woolcott to say that the exchange 8. ____________ according to plan.

"They didn't notice the missing money?"

"We 9. ________ that later."

At Scotland Yard a group of people, including Sir Reginald, asked him questions about the kidnapping.

"I was picked up outside my pub, the Vickie, and taken somewhere I'd never been before. I was kept in a dark room the whole time; they left the door open about an hour a day so I could get a little light and fresh air. The rest of the time it was dark."

"How many people did you see?"

"There were three."

"Could you identify them if you were to see them again?"

"Possibly. It was dark the whole time, so I couldn't see them that clearly."

"You say that you don't know where you were?"

"No idea. They kept me blindfolded after they kidnapped me until they put me in that room and they blindfolded me again this morning before taking out of the room – and I was blindfolded until we got out of the car at the park where those two people picked me up.

"Inspector Hudson and Junior Inspector Dinsmore."

"Yes, them."

"How long was the ride from the pub to where you were held?"

"I've no idea," Award answered.

"How long was the drive this morning?" Hudson asked.

"About 25 minutes."

"Wasn't it the same as last Thursday when you were kidnapped?"

"I suppose it was. Why are you asking me so many questions, as if I'm the one who committed some sort of crime?"

"We want to catch the people responsible for kidnapping you."

Award said, "I just want to go home."

"Call the doctor in," Sir Reginald said.

Übung 87: Welche Wörter haben eine ähnliche Bedeutung? Ordnen Sie zu!

1. question	☐ 6 arrest
2. ride	☐ liable
3. commit	☐ obligate
4. require	☐ offence
5. responsible	☐ interrogate
6. catch	☐ 2 journey
7. crime	☐ perform

A man of about forty appeared, dressed in white. “Come with me please.” He led Award out of the room. Another inspector accompanied them.

“He’s not telling the truth or not the whole truth,” Hudson said.

“He’s not being cooperative,” Sir Reginald said, “but we can’t do anything about that. He is, after all, the one who was kidnapped.”

“So we have to just let him go?”

“We have to just let him go.”

Award was gone about 45 minutes and when he came back he said he wanted to leave.

“What’s his condition?” Sir Reginald asked the doctor.

“He seems in fine condition, considering what he’s just been through. He’s not malnourished. He needs a bath. In general, he’s fine. He has a temper, but I reckon he had that before he was kidnapped. There’s no medical reason to hold him.”

“Well, Award, there you have it. You are free to go. If you think of any details that you have left out, anything you want to change, just let Inspector Hudson know. Do you have his card? We’re going to need your help to capture your kidnappers, so anything you can tell us, however small or unimportant it may seem, will be helpful.”

Award left five minutes later, escorted outside by Hudson.

Übung 88: Ordnen Sie die Berufe der jeweiligen Tätigkeit zu!

1. A doctor	[2] works in administration.
2. A CEO	[4] works in public relations.
3. A scientist	[5] works in the finance department.
4. A publicist	[3] works in R&D.
5. An accountant	[1] works in a hospital.

"Have you wrapped everything up?" Sir Reginald asked over the phone.
"No, unfortunately not."
"Good. I was about to tell you that this was your first case where you didn't get your man."
"As they say in America, Sir Reginald, 'It ain't over till it's over.'"
"You spent far too much time there, Hudson."
"Miss Paddington thinks so too."
"Keep me posted of your progress."

Übung 89: Welche Bedeutung haben folgende Redewendungen? Kreuzen Sie an!

1. Have you wrapped everything up?
   - a) [x] Are you finished?
   - b) [ ] Are you tired?
   - c) [ ] Are you ready for Christmas?

2. I'm as pleased as Punch.
   - a) [ ] I'm angry.
   - b) [x] I'm extremely happy with the way things worked out.
   - c) [ ] I like this drink a lot.

3. I don't want to hurt her feelings.
   a) ☐ I don't want to injure her feelings.
   b) ☐ I don't want to upset her.
   c) ☐ I don't want to tell her the truth.

4. I'll pop by in a little while.
   a) ☐ I'll come by with a note of warning.
   b) ☐ I'll come in the back door.
   c) ☐ I'll come to your flat in about half an hour.

"Would you like to join me and see what happens next, Dinsmore, or do you have a date tonight?"
"I don't have time for dates, Inspector Hudson. I have a job that's more than a career. It's about people's lives. I don't have time for the rest."
"You know, Dinsmore, you remind me of someone – I don't know who, and I'm afraid I don't want to know."

Hudson and Dinsmore walked back to the Bentley.
"You love your car, don't you?" she asked. Hudson nodded. "Why don't you get one of those sports cars A&L makes? A Bentley's nice, but somehow it also seems to be a car for –" she stopped speaking.
"A car for –?" Hudson said, encouraging her to finish her sentence.
"For older people."
"Dinsmore, is a BMW or a Porsche or an MG for old people?"
"That's who you usually see driving them."
"Because they're the only ones who can afford them. But they're for young people too. A Bentley is more than a car, Dinsmore. It's a way of life. It's not for old or stuffy people – you were going to say 'stuffy', I know it – it's a car for people who feel that somehow

the world should be better. Remember, the person makes the car special not the other way around. Driving a sports car won't make you trendy; it doesn't prove you have good taste."

"Men just love to get philosophical about their cars – about cars and football and pubs."

"We're going to have to park a little way away from The Dickens because Ms Jones knows this car," Hudson said, ignoring Dinsmore's last comment. "It's about twenty to five. I'm going to give Woolcott a call."

Hudson dialled the number.

"Woolcott."

"Hudson here. Are you in your office?"

"Yes, of course," he answered.

"Do you have any plans for this evening?"

"I plan on working until about 6 o'clock and then going home and fixing myself a stiff drink."

"Come down to The Dickens on the Strand."

"Why, is this your way of apologizing for your behaviour?"

"Not at all, Mr Woolcott. I just think you might see something interesting. It may or may not explain my behaviour."

"Well – Have a good evening Madeline – so where were we?"

"You were saying goodbye to Ms Jones and I was inviting you to meet me at The Dickens in about twenty-five minutes or so."

"I've had a stressful day and a nice glass of Scotch sounds much better than dinner or a drink with you, no offence intended."

"None taken. Just the same I think it might be worth your while to join me. You see, the case isn't quite closed."

"You have Award."

"Award is free, but a kidnapping is never closed until the money is returned. And there are other issues that remain open as well."

"I'm not sure, Inspector."

"Mr Woolcott, I believe you will find it time well spent."
"Okay. I have a couple of things to do, but then I'll meet you, Inspector."
"Don't take too long, Mr Woolcott. Time is running out."
They decided on a place to meet not far from The Dickens.
"Ms Jones is just leaving," Hudson said to Dinsmore, "so she's going to be a bit late. I hope that John Franklin will wait."
"I think he'll give her at least half an hour. He sounded anxious to speak with her yesterday."

Übung 90: Setzen Sie die richtigen Präpositionen ein!

ÜBUNG 90 !

1. Everything depends __________ Inspector Hudson.
2. Dinsmore did not look forward __________ an interesting afternoon __________ Hudson.
3. Did Award try to break free __________ his kidnappers?
4. The bikers went __________ a short ride.
5. They had to decide __________ a price.

Hudson and Dinsmore found a place where they could observe people entering The Dickens. The Strand was busy with people going home and people searching for a pub for an after-work drink. Hudson and Dinsmore sat among a group of people watching people and the world pass by. Franklin was the first to enter, right on time. About twenty minutes later, they saw Jones go in.
"I'd better go and find Woolcott. If they're not there when I get back, I'll be buying the CEO dinner. Do you want to come or stay here?"
"I'll stay. If they leave I can follow, if they don't go too far."

Übung 91: Ordnen Sie die Buchstaben zu einem sinnvollen Wort!

Woolcott drove up in an AS9, one of A&L's (1. csssclai) classics.

"You drive one of your own cars?"

"Naturally. It's a bad sign if a CEO of an automobile (2. amfrruuctane) manufacture drives a car made by the competition."

"A Jaguar, for instance, is not the (3. cpnoottiime) competition?"

"It depends on how you define 'competition'."

"So I've heard."

"But I drive something else on the (4. wdneeke) weekend and in the winter when the (5. wahtree) weather is bad. But in weather like this, there's no excuse for (6. dgnviir) driving something else. So, what's this about?"

"Dinner at The Dickens."

"You're taking me to dinner?"

"We'll see if it gets that far."

"Inspector Hudson, I'm not sure I like your ways. You never seem to go to a subject directly. Or you haven't with me. I'm a direct man, Inspector. That's how I got where I am. Work like corkscrew, getting deep into a thing, but never directly. You're effective, no doubt, but I don't work the way you do."

They walked up to where Dinsmore was sitting. They crossed the street and walked into The Dickens, Hudson in the lead. He looked around. The place was full.

"As you can see, there will be a bit of a wait," a waiter said.

“It’s okay; we’re just going to say ‘Hello’ to some friends. Or I hope we are.” Hudson looked and looked. Finally in a dark corner, he found them. “Dinsmore, you didn’t notice him?”
“I did, sir, I just thought I’d let you enjoy the surprise.”
“Right this way, Mr Woolcott,” and Hudson led the two through the busy restaurant to a quiet table in the back, where the light didn’t shine too brightly, where people could be forgotten, if they sought to be alone among the crowd. Hudson walked slowly. The three were in conversation, heads tilted down.

Übung 92: Setzen Sie, wenn nötig, den bestimmten oder unbestimmten Artikel ein!

1. The biker looked forward to a long stay in ______ hospital.
2. Dinsmore sat across ______ street from The Dickens.
3. Inspector Hudson went to ______ restaurant in London.
4. In ______ back of the restaurant sat Madeline Jones.
5. She went to work at ______ A&L.
6. Donald Award worked at ______ automobile producer.

Hudson led them right up to the table. Award stood.
“Sit, Mr Award,” said Hudson.
Suddenly, Jones saw Woolcott, and she too stood.
“Sit, Ms Jones,” Hudson said to her. “And you too, Mr Franklin.”
“Who are you?” Franklin asked.
“Inspector Hudson, Scotland Yard,” Jones answered.
“Well you should be arresting that man,” Award said, standing and pointing at Woolcott. “He’s the one who had me kidnapped.”
“I had you kidnapped? Why I’d like to take you outside, Award, and

give you the thrashing you deserve. If your work wasn't so good I'd have thrashed you years ago and thrown you out of my company."
Hudson and Woolcott looked at the three sitting in their chairs. Dinsmore got a few more chairs and they all sat down together.
"So, Franklin, this is an unorthodox approach to recruiting engineers," Hudson said.
"Good evening," Franklin said, preparing to leave.
"Don't make me pull rank on you, Mr Franklin."
"Rank?"
"Yes, you're a CEO and I'm a Scotland Yard Inspector. At the races, we're all equals, with our betting slips. At the opera, you'd get the better seats, no doubt. At the moment, you have to do what I say."
"Nobody talks to me like that!"
"We can talk here like gentlemen, or we can go to Scotland Yard and talk. Your choice, Mr Franklin." Franklin sat silently. "So, Ms Jones, would you like to explain what happened?"
"No," she said, almost happily.

ÜBUNG 93 !

Übung 93: Sind folgende Aussagen richtig? Markieren Sie mit richtig ✔ oder falsch – !

1. Donald Award thinks Woolcott had him kidnapped. ☐
2. Madeline Jones is agreeably surprised by Inspector Hudson's appearance in the restaurant. ☐
3. Franklin feels superior to Inspector Hudson. ☐
4. Woolcott congratulates Franklin on his recruitment technique. ☐
5. Everyone at the table is cooperative. ☐
6. Award's accusation didn't take Woolcott by surprise. ☐

"Then I'll try. Feel free to correct me. You told Franklin about the new engine, who decided he would like to have a new engineer. You wanted to provide that engineer, but at a charge. Then you had to figure out how to get Award to go to Franklin's willingly. He's a bit old to be a problem-child, but he is one nonetheless. So, you watched as he threatened and complained. You are Woolcott's eyes and ears, so you knew what was going on. Award demands a pay rise but doesn't know he's going to get it and he threatens to take his ideas elsewhere. He gets kidnapped before he finds out about the pay rise and before he can finish his project. Naturally, the kidnappers tell him that they're working for Woolcott and Donleavy. In fact, they're friends of Donleavy's, so it looks like he's involved. Award doesn't know what's going to happen. You never think that maybe they're going to kill you. They call Woolcott and demand money, which never strikes you as strange. The money they demand is their payment for kidnapping you. They keep you at the A&L castle in Hertfordshire, and it's like being 'at home'. Only you're not at home, and you're not happy. You are unhappy, and you make your kidnappers unhappy. You say you'll never work for A&L again, but just to keep you quiet Jones offers you a pay-off, hence the ransom doubles overnight. What is Jones getting out of all of this? She's getting a 'finder's fee' from Franklin. Any laws broken yet? We have kidnapping and extortion and money paid for an illegal action. The bikers are probably riding on stolen motorcycles. Trespassing and illegal entry – the castle was not exactly being used for company business, Ms Jones. These are just some of the charges. Need I go on?"

Übung 94: Formulieren Sie die Sätze in der indirekten Rede!

1. "I was kidnapped," he said.

He said ______________________________

2. "You wanted to provide that engineer, but at a charge," he said.

____

3. "I'll never work for A&L again," he said.

____

4. "You told Franklin about the new engine," he said.

____

5. "I have suspected the wrong person all along," he said.

____

"I think we're at the point where you tell us exactly what you want," Franklin said.

"It's not as easy as that," Hudson said. "You see, not one of you is innocent. Award was kidnapped and then bought. He came here expecting part of the ransom. My question is, where's the money?"

"It's not here," Jones said, dryly.

"You were supposed to bring me £50,000," Award nearly shouted. "Let's see the money, Ms Jones."

"Really, I don't have it."

"Yes, you do," Hudson said. "Put your handbag on the table." Ms Jones made no move to comply. "Do you want me to call the bobbies? We can take you out of here like a common criminal or we can do it my way. You choose."

Jones put her handbag on the table.

Hudson opened her bag. Inside were packets of £20 notes.

"Let's all of us quietly get up and leave. Franklin, please pay."

Hudson pulled out his mobile phone and called Scotland Yard.

"Please send a van around, will you, for three. Yes, I'll follow."

Franklin acted as if he were not part of the group.

"I'm sure your money is in here, too, so you'll want to come with us," Hudson said.

"Is there any reason for Award to go?" Woolcott asked. "The lad has had quite a day already."

"I agree. But he used poor judgement. He could learn a bit from his friend Malcolm Evans. We'll go easy on him."

"How did you know that somebody at A&L was involved?" Woolcott asked.

"I only knew for certain, Mr Woolcott, when the kidnappers called me 'Inspector' over the phone. Ms Jones, I think your days as a head-hunter are over. How much money did Franklin pay you?"

Ms Jones smiled at Hudson. It was the smile that might cross a snake's face just before it swallows a frog whole. "More than A&L paid for Award," she whispered, but it was the kind of whisper the frog hears before the jaws of the snake unlock.

Übung 95: Übersetzen Sie folgende Wörter!

1. attorney ______
2. judge Gesetz
3. intention ______
4. illegal ______
5. court Gericht
6. defendant ______
7. defender ______

She stepped away from the table. Her hand went for the handbag, but Hudson was quicker, and he pulled the bag out of her grasp. He reached inside and found a pistol.

Dinsmore stood looking at her, determined but not challenging.

"Let's go," Hudson said, quietly and calmly.

ÜBUNG 96 !

Übung 96: Beantworten Sie die Fragen zum Text!

1. Who started everything?

____

2. When did Hudson realize Woolcott wasn't involved?

____

3. How did he find out that Award wanted money?

____

4. Why was Award kept at A&L's castle?

____

5. What was Franklin's role in everything?

____

Several days later.

"I think Junior Inspector Dinsmore has a fine career ahead of her, Sir Reginald, but she needs to rethink some of her priorities."

"Really, why do you say that?"

"She's far too hard on people in general. She has no social life. She has to do more than simply be an inspector. If you want to be good at this profession, you can't just be an inspector."

"Interesting that you should say that. You see, I reassigned Johnson and Harrison after she requested to be assigned to you."

"She wanted to be assigned to me?"

"Indeed. She finds your approach well-suited to hers. In fact, she sees you as a mentor. She has asked me about you and I have told her the little I know. I think what you see when you look at young Dinsmore is young Hudson. The difference is, besides the blonde hair, she has a real kick."

"Sir Reginald. I'm going to pretend I didn't hear that."

Abschlusstest

Übung 1: Setzen Sie die Wörter in Klammern in die Lücken ein!
(opportunities, promotion, strengths, sacked, development, weaknesses, competition, report, threats, headquarters)

1. Some engineers were responsible for product ____________.
2. He was ____________ because his job performance was poor.
3. Two companies that produce the same product are in ____________ for customers.
4. The CEO's office is always in the ____________.
5. Because he did his job so well, he received a ____________ at the end of the year.
6. A SWOT analysis consists of ____________, ____________, ____________ and ____________.
7. Every year, A&L publishes an annual ____________.

Übung 2: Welches Wort ist das „schwarze Schaf"?

1. Accounts, R&D, Sales, Men's
2. to argue, to promote, to discuss, to exchange views
3. confidential, convert, secret, private
4. polite, tactful, helpful, diplomatic
5. report, letter, email, filing cabinet
6. agent, CEO, manager, foreman

Übung 3: Formen Sie die Sätze ins Passiv um!

1. Donald Award developed a new engine for A&L.

____

2. Award held Jack Donleavy responsible for slowing his project.

____

3. Madeline Jones developed a plan.

____

4. Bikers kidnapped Donald Award.

____

5. Hudson and Dinsmore found Donald Award.

____

6. Award was working on an important project.

____

Übung 4: Bringen Sie die Sätze und Fragen in die richtige Reihenfolge!

1. employee difficult Donald Award a was

Was Donald Award a difficult employee?

2. assistant Martin Madeline is Jones Woolcott's

Madeline Jones is Martin Woolcott's assistant.

3. progress making new are with any you your engine?

____

4. lot competition A&L a of has

A&L has a lot of competition.

5. outside Mr Award kidnapped pub a right was

6. led Jack Donleavy R&D the was Department by

7. computer monitors IT the systems Department and and software develops

Übung 5: Wie heißt die Formulierung auf Englisch?

1. jemanden ernst nehmen ______
2. jemanden von einem Projekt abziehen ______
3. Formulare ausfüllen ______
4. alles abstreiten ______
5. Firmenspionage ______
6. Aktenschränke ______
7. Durchwahl ______
8. Verkaufsleiterin ______
9. Konkurrenz ______

Übung 6: Setzen Sie die richtigen Präpositionen ein!

1. Award was _____ the point _____ leaving this company.
2. There was nothing _____ show _____ all their hard work.
3. He took _____ too much work.
4. Hudson showed _____ at the castle unannounced.
5. Hudson and Dinsmore had to decide _____ two alternatives.
6. Award was a good advertisement _____ his company.

Übung 7: Welche Bedeutung haben folgende Redewendungen? Kreuzen Sie an!

1. I'm of two minds on this subject.
   a) ☐ I can't make up my mind about this subject.
   b) ☐ I agree with my two colleagues.
   c) ☐ I do know what I think of this.

2. I've had enough! Put a sock in it!
   a) ☐ Do the laundry.
   b) ☐ Stop talking.
   c) ☐ I cannot eat any more.

3. You're going to pay!
   a) ☐ You'll be sorry for what you've done.
   b) ☐ I bought the last round.
   c) ☐ It's your round.

4. If you don't mind, I'm going to get back to work.
   a) ☐ I'm going to start working again.

b) ☐ If you don't want me to, I won't do the work.
c) ☐ If you have nothing to do, I'll start working again.

5. Have you wrapped everything up?
a) ☐ Are you ready for dinner?
b) ☐ Are you finished?
c) ☐ Are you ready for Christmas?

Übung 8: Formulieren Sie die Sätze in der indirekten Rede!

1. "I'll pick up the tickets tomorrow morning at 7.30," he said.

____

2. "The children have been a lot of trouble," she said.

____

3. "Do you have any idea where you were held?," he asked.

____

4. "This will be the last time we see each other," she said.

____

5. "Woolcott told me the money was missing," he said.

____

6. "Franklin gave me more money than Woolcott did," she said.

____

7. "I'm trying to find a missing engineer," he said.

____

Übung 9: Wie antwortet man kurz und höflich?

1. How are you?
   a) ☐ Not bad. And you?
   b) ☐ My life is a mess. My cat has just died and my boss is a fool.
   c) ☐ Terrible. How are you?

2. Nice to see you!
   a) ☐ See you!
   b) ☐ You too.
   c) ☐ Nice to see you, too.

3. Are you Martin Woolcott?
   a) ☐ No.
   b) ☐ Mr Woolcott is older than me.
   c) ☐ No, I'm not.

Übung 10: Bringen Sie die Sätze des Telefonats in die richtige Reihenfolge!

1. "I'll put you through."
2. "A&L Headquarters."
3. "Could you give me his extension first?"
4. "Thank you."
5. "Yes, it's 4715. I'll put you through now."
6. "May I speak with Mr Donleavy?"

Lösung: _ _ _ _ _ _

Lösungen

Übung 1: 1. engineer 2. pay rise 3. promotion 4. keep out of the red 5. sacked 6. pension 7. making a fortune
Übung 2: 1. economically 2. engine 3. reputation 4. function 5. maintain 6. period 7. hours at a time 8. breakthrough
Übung 3: 1. unknown 2. amazon 3. impression 4. glory 5. mentor
Übung 4: 1. to take somebody seriously 2. to come up with something 3. to give credit to somebody 4. to take somebody off a project 5. to bring somebody onto a project 6. to take care of something
Übung 5: 1. b, d, m, n 2. c, e, f, g, j, l 3. a, h, k
Übung 6: 1. advise 2. adviser 3. advisable 4. advisory 5. advised 6. advice
Übung 7: 1. CEO 2. engineer 3. senior engineer 4. director of Research and Development 5. racing driver
Übung 8: 1. advertising 2. advertiser 3. advert 4. advertisement 5. advertised
Übung 9: 1. for 2. on 3. that 4. to 5. between 6. against 7. about
Übung 10: 1. matter 2. avoided 3. designing 4. competition 5. permission 6. consequences
Übung 11: 1. richtig 2. falsch 3. richtig 4. falsch 5 richtig 6. richtig 7. falsch
Übung 12: 1. Donleavy reported to Mr Woolcott that Award had denied everything. 2. Woolcott demanded that Donleavy keep his people under control. 3. He threatened to find another head/director for the Research and Development department. 4. After the call he went/walked angrily to his people in the workshop. 5. Hudson hated filling in forms. 6. He had a lot of paperwork to do that morning.
Übung 13: 2. Sir Reginald reported that a young man had turned up missing. 3. Hudson asked if Jennifer was giving him problems. 4. Sir Reginald asked if he could continue. 5. Sir Reginald said that the young man had been gone a week.
Übung 14: 1. corporate espionage 2. square letters 3. kidnapping 4. engine 5. ransom 6. deception
Übung 15: 1. The letter was sent back to the addressee. 2. The vagabond was removed by the security guard. 3. The security guard was surprised by the vagrant. 4. The letter on the lobby floor was noticed by the guard. 5. Large sums are paid by sports car enthusiasts for their cars.
Übung 16: 1. führte/led 2. ziemlich/rather 3. Ingenieur/engineer 4. entführt/kidnapped 5. kürzlich/recently 6. Grund/reason 7. Vergangenheitsform/past tense 8. irgendwie/somehow
Übung 17: 1. Does anybody have an idea who might have kidnapped him? 2. Does Mr Woolcott know how long Award has been missing? 3. Why did you

hesitate to call the police? 4. Has Award ever taken time off without telling anybody? 5. Did anybody go by his flat to see if he was home? 6. Why do you speak of Award in the past tense all the time?

Übung 18: 1. on show 2. shown up 3. showed … around 4. take … down 5. nothing to show 6. took on 7. took over

Übung 19: 1. fax machine 2. printer 3. filing cabinets 4. typewriter 5. area 6. secretary

Übung 20: 1. colleagues 2. introduce 3. attempt 4. explain 5. behaviour 6. convincing

Übung 21: 1. had a point 2. at the point of 3. pointed out 4. at the point of no return 5. to the point of 6. makes a point of 7. point of view

Übung 22: 1. extension 2. directories 3. programs 4. letters 5. requests 6. items 7. projects 8. emails

Übung 23: 1. You can call me at any time. My extension is 6478. 2. Hudson looked through all the directories and files on Award's computer. 3. Marvin Good introduced himself to Hudson. 4. How much money are the kidnappers demanding? 5. It was only a brief call. 6. Ms Jagger put the caller through.

Übung 24: 2. Hudson picked up the phone on Award's desk and handed it to Donleavy. 3. Woolcott sat in his office waiting for a call. 4. Hudson went back to Award's office holding a cup of coffee in his hand. 5. The man waved his hand while making a funny face into the camera. 6. Malcolm Evans walked in and greeted Hudson.

Übung 25: 1. down 2. harder 3. for 4. place 5. delivery 6. times

Übung 26: 1. in 2. to 3. for 4. around 5. into 6. next to

Übung 27: 1. New ideas are constantly developed by engineers. 2. A creative atmosphere was provided by the company. 3. He was offered a new position by A&L. 4. Award's ambitious project wasn't valued by A&L. 5. Corrections can be done easier with a computer than with a typewriter.

Übung 28: 1. in 2. around 3. across 4. work 5. whether 6. answering 7. businessmen 8. out 9. for

Übung 29: 1. beyond ... means 2. by means of 3. by no means 4. at all means 5. within … means

Übung 30: 1. IT 2. Sales & Marketing 3. Personnel/Human Resources 4. Public Relations 5. Accounts

Übung 31: 1. Sales and Marketing are two separate departments at A&L. 2. Who is in charge in the Sales Department? 3. The secretary gave Hudson the name of the sales manager/the person in charge of the Sales Department. 4. Many sales reps/representatives work in Janet O'Malley's department. 5. If the sales manager is not in, one of her sales reps will surely help you.

Übung 32: 1. a 2. c 3. c 4. b 5. a

Übung 33: 1. companies 2. manufacturer 3. competition 4. market analysis 5. strengths 6. threats 7. specialists

Übung 34: 1. Are your cars more comfortable than the ones manufactured by VF? 2. Who is the founder of VF? 3. What do you mean by cut-throat? 4. How did the driver of the Henley insult Victor Franklin? 5. Why are VF's cars more valuable than A&L's? 6. Are A&L's sales ahead of its competitors'?

Übung 35: 1. shareholder 2. head office 3. founder 4. business card 5. market leader 6. sales figures 7. family business

Übung 36: 1. Because it was not a very inspiring place to work. 2. Because he had Award's user ID and his passwords. 3. He found out that Award's emails had been deleted. 4. Because he didn't have access to his email account. 5. Only somebody in the IT department, one of the presidents or Mr Woolcott should have been able to do that.

Übung 37: 1. Hudson wanted Charlotte Easter to give him information on A&L's competitors. 2. Hudson wanted Melanie Cook to tell him who had access to Award's emails. 3. Somebody didn't want Hudson to get any information. 4. Hudson wanted Donleavy to answer his questions. 5. Woolcott wanted the development of the new engine to be slowed down.

Übung 38: 1. twice 2. close by 3. afterwards 4. recognized 5. some

Übung 39: 1. What were you doing in my office? 2. I was just using your phone. 3. Your company was trying some rather novel tactics. 4. I was following my boss's orders. 5. I went home at seven. 6. I thought she did work that I didn't have time for.

Übung 40: 1. collects 2. president 3. brilliant 4. businessman 5. adequate 6. member

Übung 41: 1. a 2. c 3. b 4. a

Übung 42: 1. insurance policy 2. over-insured 3. insurance company 4. insurance agent 5. premium 6. insurance specialist

Übung 43: 1. They were negotiating the ransom. 2. Hudson was working on a complicated kidnapping case. 3. Business was the only thing on his mind. 4. Money is not the only reason why kidnappers take someone hostage. 5. The kidnappers were planning on killing the hostage.

Übung 44: 1. away 2. down 3. back 4. quickly 5. somewhere 6. Firstly 7. Secondly

Übung 45: 1. more successful 2. more 3. funnier 4. more violent 5. later 6. more talented

Übung 46: 1. They went to the VF headquarters in St. Albans. 2. Because VF was a competitor of A&L and they could have kidnapped Award. 3. That he was a strong and tough man. 4. No, but he thought it was possible that Donleavy's motorcycle gang took revenge on Award for Donleavy. 5. Because he was working for A&L.

Übung 47: 1. b 2. c 3. a
Übung 48: 1. negotiator 2. expertise 3. department 4. postpone 5. supremely 6. briefcase
Übung 49: 1. share prices 2. fluctuating 3. clutch 4. to release onto the market 5. investment 6. viability
Übung 50: 1. with 2. to 3. from 4. at 5. at 6. up 7. in 8. over
Übung 51: 1. a 2. a 3. c
Übung 52: 1. c 2. a 3. b 4. c
Übung 53: 1. wages 2. return 3. plant 4. salary 5. objection 6. complain
Übung 54: 1. dialled 2. reservations 3. Return 4. following 5. confirmation
Übung 55: 1. No, he's a rather difficult employee. 2. He has nothing to do. He wants more information about Award. 3. It is most definitely not diplomatic. 4. He gets numbers from Ms Jones' telephone. 5. Yes, they are supposed to remain private and confidential.
Übung 56: 1. profit 2. bill 3. confident 4. direct 5. hang up 6. impromptu
Übung 57: 2. She said she thought it was a waste of time. 3. The kidnappers said they wanted more money. 4. Evans said Award always went to a pub after work. 5. They said they would call on Monday.
Übung 58: 3, 2, 6, 5, 1, 4
Übung 59: 1. demand/insist 2. conclude/terminate 3. annoyed/irritated 4. deal/agreement 5. punctual/prompt 6. assistant/subordinate 7. proof/evidence
Übung 60: 1. message 2. extension 3. this 4. called 5. called 6. speak 7. suit 8. again
Übung 61: 1. to 2. on/with 3. for/at 4. in/across 5. to/with 6. of 7. in
Übung 62: 1. I will just call back later. 2. May I leave a message? 3. I'd like to speak with Mr Woolcott please. 4. This is Malcolm Evans in Research and Development. 5. I'm afraid he is in a meeting. 6. I have a lot of work at the moment.
Übung 63: 1. seems 2. got 3. focused 4. walked 5. set 6. took 7. returned
Übung 64: 1. What 2. Who 3. Where 4. Who 5. How 6. What
Übung 65: 1. to take time off/I need a holiday. 2. to put off/Let's postpone the meeting 3. to take off/Sales have exploded. 4. to ring off/I hung up the phone 5. to be off/I'm leaving now.
Übung 66: 1. falsch 2. falsch 3. falsch 4. richtig 5. falsch 6. richtig 7. richtig
Übung 67: 1. Verhandlungen 2. engagiert 3. Beweis 4. aggressive Verkaufstaktik 5. überreden 6. Gegenstück
Übung 68 1. Just a moment please! 2. He will just have to wait. 3. I was just about to make the sale. 4. She was speaking to him about it. 5. Just now you said the price was too low.
Übung 69: 1. climbed 2. particularly 3. rich 4. rather than 5. modern 6. examined
Übung 70: 1. always 2. better 3. anything 4. worthless 5. dangerous

Übung 71: 1. richtig 2. richtig 3. falsch 4. richtig 5. falsch
Übung 72: 1. "The only thing we don't have is women." 2. "That's a stupid idea." 3. "I'll buy a car next year." 4. "We're not going to do that." 5. "Drive to London!" 6. "I can deliver the hostage by Thursday."
Übung 73: 1. b 2. a 3. c
Übung 74: 1. The golf caddy suggested a six iron. 2. The captain of the ship waved to the passengers. 3. Maybe there would be presents and cocktails, perhaps some hors d'oeuvres. 4. Did I mention that I'm a stamp collector?
Übung 75: 1. b 2. a 3. b 4. b 5. b
Übung 76: 3, 5, 2, 7, 1, 6, 4
Übung 77: 1. He wants to make things difficult for the kidnappers. 2. Woolcott's secretary, Ms Jagger, mentions it over the phone to an employee and Hudson overhears her. 3. He hears Donald Award's voice. 4. Yes, they do meet one of the bikers.
Übung 78: 1. defend/condemn 2. threaten/protect 3. savoury/sweet 4. deny/acknowledge 5. develop/reduce 6. question/reply 7. complicated/straightforward
Übung 79: 1. fancy 2. time 3. executive 4. desk 5. meeting 6. story 7. control
Übung 80: 1. "You never checked the safe?" 2. "Does anyone else have access to the safe?" 3. Ms Jagger came in quickly. 4. "Did you open the safe yesterday?" 5. "Did anyone else come into my office?"
Übung 81: 1. falsch 2. richtig 3. richtig 4. falsch 5. falsch 6. richtig
Übung 82: 1. blodshed (bloodshed) 2. wholes (holes) 3. man (men) 4. of (off) 5. meat (meet) 6. best (rest) 7. Canibal's (Carnibal's)
Übung 83: 1. rode 2. direction 3. walked 4. stopped 5. looked 6. helmets 7. could
Übung 84: 1. a 2. b 3. b 4. b
Übung 85: 1. kneeled 2. untied 3. untied 4. stand up 5. looked over 6. get out of 7. walking 8. come 9. lead the way 10. got to his feet 11. joined 12. opened 13. got in
Übung 86: 1. know 2. came 3. try 4. find out 5. accompanied 6. followed 7. report 8. had gone 9. will discuss
Übung 87: question/interrogate 2. ride/journey 3. commit/perform 4. require/obligate 5. responsible/liable 6. catch/arrest 7. crime/offence
Übung 88: 1. A doctor works in a hospital. 2. A CEO works in administration. 3. A scientist works in R&D. 4. A publicist works in public relations. 5. An accountant works in the finance department.
Übung 89: 1. a 2. b 3. b 4. c
Übung 90: 1. on/upon 2. to, with 3. from/of 4. for/on 5. on/upon
Übung 91: 1. classics 2. manufacturer 3. competition 4. weekend 5. weather 6. driving
Übung 92: 1. – 2. the 3. a 4. the 5. – 6. an
Übung 93: 1. richtig 2. falsch 3. richtig 4. falsch 5. falsch 6. falsch

Übung 94: 1. He said he was kidnapped. 2. He said you had wanted to provide that engineer, but at a charge. 3. He said he would never work for A&L again. 4. He said you had told Franklin about the new engine. 5. He said he had suspected the wrong person all along.
Übung 95: 1. Rechtsanwalt 2. Richter 3. Absicht 4. rechtswidrig 5. Gericht 6. Beklagter/Angeklagter 7. Verteidiger
Übung 96: 1. Ms Jones when she saw Award was unhappy. 2. He realized Woolcott was not involved when Woolcott was surprised at the missing money. 3. Hudson overheard the bikers say that he was involved. 4. He was kept at the castle to make it appear that A&L had kidnapped him. 5. He gave Ms Jones money to provide him with a new engineer, Award.

Lösungen Abschlusstest

Übung 1: 1. development 2. sacked 3. competition 4. headquarters 5. promotion 6. strengths, weaknesses, opportunities, threats 7. report
Übung 2: 1. Men's 2. to promote 3. convert 4. helpful 5. filing cabinet 6. agent
Übung 3: A new engine was developed for A&L by Donald Award. 2. Jack Donleavy was held responsible by Award for slowing his project. 3. A plan was developed by Madeline Jones. 4. Donald Award was kidnapped by bikers. 5. Donald Award was found by Hudson and Dinsmore. 6. An important project was being worked on by Award.
Übung 4: 1. Donald Award was a difficult employee. 2. Madeline Jones is Martin Woolcott's assistant. 3. Are you making any progress with your new engine? 4. A&L has a lot of competition. 5. Mr Award was kidnapped right outside a pub. 6. The R&D Department was led by Jack Donleavy. 7. The IT Department monitors and develops computer systems and software.
Übung 5: 1. to take someone seriously 2. to take someone off a project 3. to fill in forms 4. to deny everything 5. corporate espionage 6. filing cabinet 7. extension 8. sales manager/director 9. competition
Übung 6: 1. on/at, of 2. to, for 3. on 4. up 5. between 6. for
Übung 7: 1. a 2. b 3. a 4. a 5. b
Übung 8: 1. He said that he would pick up the tickets tomorrow morning at 7.30. 2. She said that the children had been a lot of trouble. 3. He asked if he/she had any idea where he/she was held. 4. She said that it would be the last time we saw each other. 5. He said that Woolcott had told him the money was missing. 6. She said that Franklin had given her more money than Woolcott did. 7. He said that he was trying to find a missing engineer.
Übung 9: 1. a 2. c 3. c
Übung 10: 2, 6, 1, 3, 5, 4